Translation of the

Memorial Book of Yampol

Ayara be-lehavot
Pinkas Yampola
Pelekh Volyn

A City in Flames
Yizkor Book of Yampol, Ukraine
(District of Volhyn)

Edited by: Leon Gellman
Originally Published in Hebrew and Yiddish
Jerusalem, 1963

Published by JewishGen

An Affiliate of the Museum of Jewish Heritage - A Living Memorial to the Holocaust
New York

Translation of: *Ayara be-lehavot, Pinkas Yampola, Pelekh Volyn*

A City in Flames
Yizkor (Memorial) Book of Yampol, Ukraine
(District of Volhyn)

Copyright © 2013 by JewishGen, Inc.
All rights reserved.
Second Printing: June 2013, Tammuz 5773

Translation Project Coordinator: Judy Wolkovitch
Layout: Joel Alpert
Image Editor: Jan R. Fine
Cover Design: Jan R. Fine
Publicity: Sandra Hirschhorn

Published by JewishGen, Inc.
An Affiliate of the Museum of Jewish Heritage
A Living Memorial to the Holocaust
36 Battery Place, New York, NY 10280

"JewishGen, Inc. is not responsible for inaccuracies or omissions in the original work and makes no representations regarding the accuracy of this translation. Digital images of the original book's contents can be seen online at the New York Public Library Web site."

The mission of the JewishGen organization is to produce a translation of the original work and we cannot verify the accuracy of statements or alter facts cited.

Printed in the United States of America by Lightning Source, Inc.

Library of Congress Control Number (LCCN): 2013932633
ISBN: 978-1-939561-02-2 (hard cover: 184 pages, alk. paper)

JewishGen and the Yizkor Books in Print Project

This book has been published by the **Yizkor Books in Print Project,** as part of the **Yizkor Book Project** of JewishGen, Inc.

JewishGen, Inc. is a non-profit organization founded in 1987 as a resource for Jewish genealogy. Its website [www.jewishgen.org] serves as an international clearinghouse and resource center to assist individuals who are researching the history of their Jewish families and the places where they lived. JewishGen provides databases, facilitates discussion groups, and coordinates projects relating to Jewish genealogy and the history of the Jewish people. In 2003, JewishGen became an affiliate of the **Museum of Jewish Heritage - A Living Memorial to the Holocaust** in New York.

The **JewishGen Yizkor Book Project** was organized to make more widely known the existence of Yizkor (Memorial) Books written by survivors and former residents of various Jewish communities throughout the world. Later, volunteers connected to the different destroyed communities began cooperating to have these books translated from the original language—usually Hebrew or Yiddish—into English, thus enabling a wider audience to have access to the valuable information contained within them. As each chapter of these books was translated, it was posted on the JewishGen website and made available to the general public.

The **Yizkor Books in Print Project** began in 2011 as an initiative to print and publish Yizkor Books that had been fully translated, so that hard copies would be available for purchase by the descendants of these communities and also by scholars, universities, synagogues, libraries, and museums.

These Yizkor books have been produced almost entirely through the volunteer effort of researchers from around the world, assisted by donations from private individuals. The books are printed and sold at near cost, so as to make them as affordable as possible. Our goal is to make this important genre of Jewish literature and history available in English in book form, so that people can have the personal histories of their ancestral towns on their bookshelves for themselves and for their children and grandchildren.

A list of all published translated Yizkor Books can be found at:
http://www.jewishgen.org/Yizkor/ybip.html

Lance Ackerfeld, Yizkor Book Project Manager

Joel Alpert, Yizkor Book in Print Project Coordinator

JewishGen
Yizkor Book Project

This book is presented by the
Yizkor Books in Print Project
Project Coordinator: Joel Alpert

Part of the
Yizkor Books Project of JewishGen, Inc.
Project Manager: Lance Ackerfeld

These books have been produced solely through volunteer effort of individuals from around the world. The books are printed and sold at near cost, so as to make them as affordable as possible.

Our goal is to make this history and important genre of Jewish literature available in English in book form so that people can have the near-personal histories of their ancestral towns on their book-shelves for themselves and for their children and grandchildren.

Any donations to the Yizkor Books Project are appreciated.

Please send donations to:
Yizkor Book Project
JewishGen
36 Battery Place
New York, NY 10280

JewishGen, Inc. is an affiliate of the
Museum of Jewish Heritage
A Living Memorial to the Holocaust

Title Page of Original Yiddish and Hebrew Yizkor Book

עיירה בלהבות

פנקס יאמפאלא

(פלך והלין)

מוקדש אל הקדושים והטהורים, אנשי העיירה, שנרצחו ונטבחו
על ידי מרצחי עמנו ימח שמם וזכרם. שפך עליהם זעמך
וחרון אפך ישיגם !

ב ע ר י כ ת
אריה ליב גלמן

בסיוע יד ושם רשות הזכרון לשואת ולגבורה, ירושלים, הר הזכרון
והקונגרס היהודי העולמי

Translation of the Title Page of Original Yizkor Book

A CITY IN FLAMES

MEMORIAL BOOK OF YAMPOL

(DISTRICT OF VOLHYN)

Dedicated to the memory of the decent, honest, G-d fearing people of the city who were killed and massacred by the slaughterers of our nation. May the memory of the slaughterers be wiped out from the face of the earth. We pray that G-d should pour His wrath upon them and His anger should reach them wherever they are.

EDITED BY

Arieh Leib Gellman
Jerusalem

Head of the Commemoration Committee
for the town, with the assistance of
Yad Vashem and The World Jewish Congress
1963

(Hebrew and Yiddish)

CO-EDITORS:

Ezriel - Son of Baruch Goren (Pardes Chana)
David - Son of Yitzhak Rubin (Kfar Chassidim)

Foreword for the Translation

This translation was undertaken as a tribute to our ancestors and their friends and relatives who lived in Yampol. I would like to acknowledge those who contributed to this project:

Dayan Berkovitz, Max and Ruth Davis, Michael Davis, Rael Davis, Al and Lynn Finkel, Irwin and Molly Fridovich, Judy and Michael Green, Brian and Evie Hill, Alvin and Pearl Holzberg, Jay Lenefsky, David Lewin, Roland Rance, Cynthia Shaw, Clare Schwartz, Harvey and Esther Sonin, Inbar Tamari and especially to Rabbi David Shapiro in Jerusalem who edited and translated large sections of this book.

When I took upon myself the task of organizing the translation of this book I had no idea of what it contained. My mother, of blessed memory, had told me a few stories about her difficult life in Yampol and I had drawn the conclusion that Yampol was a tiny shtetl where simple good hearted people lived and struggled. I had no idea of the depth of learning and intellect that existed there. The pages of this book encompass the learned, the whimsical, the horrifying, the joy - the total gamut of emotion that is human life. Putting it together was a very moving experience and the rewards have far exceeded my expectations.

As organizer and typist I apologize for any errors. The sections were translated by many people and some of the sections are a summary of the material rather than a literal word by word translation of the text. The aim of this book is to enable the reader to know what the original contains. Some of the material was exceedingly difficult and some of it is a translation from the Hebrew that had already been translated from Yiddish. The list of the names of the martyred has been included both in Hebrew and English because the spellings are not always easy to transliterate but I wanted it to be accessible to those who do not read Hebrew.

Certain phrases and names have asterisks and numbers by them. You will find a list of notations at the end of the book.

This book is an epitaph to the memories of the many who perished and I hope this translation will allow more people to appreciate the beauties and the hardships of our ancestors.

April 1998

In loving memory, Judy Wolkovitch

YAMPOL

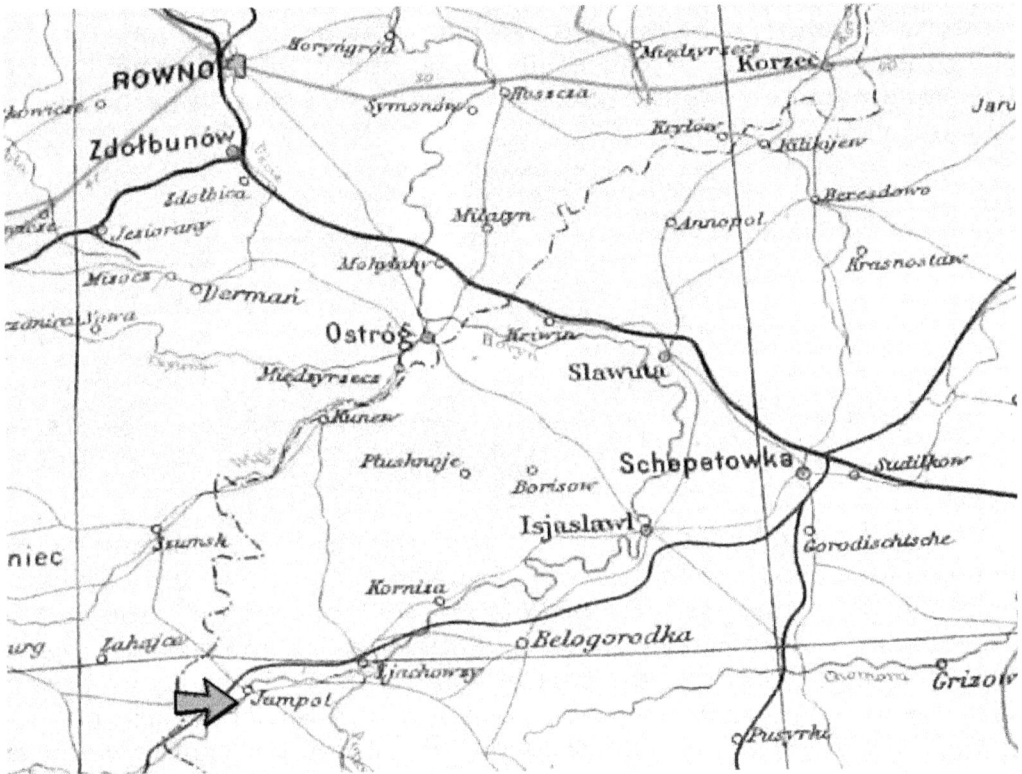

YAMPOL (Jampol), Ukraine, 49°58' N 26°15' E , 308 km W of Kiev,

Title: **Deutsch-Russisches Grenzgebiet : Ubersichtskarte 1:1,000,000**

Place of publication: **Berlin**

Publisher: **Generstab der Luftwaffe**

Date: **1938**

Courtesy: *The Henry J. Bruman Map Collection, Charles E. Young Research Library, UCLA*

Yampol, Volhynia Gubernia

A gubernia is a Russian Province that was ruled by a governor. It was a major administrative district that was formed under Peter the Great in the 18th century. There were a number of gubernias whose borders changed over the years and Volhynia Gubernia now lies in western Ukraine. The town of Yampol was a small shtetl on the Goryn (Horyn) River. It can easily be confused with a larger town of the same name on the Dniester River in the Podolia Gubernia which is south-east of Volhynia.

Volhynia was ruled by Poland until the late 18th century, when Poland was partitioned by the Prussian, Austrian, and Russian empires. After the partition of Poland, Volhynia was a gubernia, or province, of the Russian Empire until 1919, when the western part of Volhynia once again became part of Poland. In 1945 the entire area of the Volhynia Gubernia was absorbed into the Soviet Union, but the gubernia system was no longer used and the Volhynia name was used to identify a smaller region, called an oblast, in the western part of the old gubernia. Most of what was the Volhynia Gubernia is now in Ukraine, with a small part of northern Volhynia in Belarus. Major cities and towns in and around Volhynia include Zhitomir (the former capital), Rovno, Lutsk, Kovel, Berdichev, and Novograd-Volinsk.

Yampol lies 45 miles south of Rivne (Rovno), which is one of the major cities in Volhynia Gubernia with a population of around 21,000. According to the Encyclopedia of Jewish Life, Yampol was probably settled in the 17th century and since that time was subjected to a number of attacks over the years by marauders and armies. In 1765 the Jewish population was 476 and in 1897 the Jews numbered 1,482, over fifty per cent of the total population in the village. Yampol was occupied by the Germans in July 1941 and in the years 1941-1942 1,700 Jews from Yampol and neighboring towns were murdered. A monument has been erected to the Jews who perished in Yampol, Belogorsk and Kornitsa (see page xii.) Thus ended the Jewish community of Yampol.

A number of distinguished rabbis came from Yampol or lived there including Rabbi Yechiel Michel, the Maggid of Zlotshov and his son Reb. Yosef of Yampol. Rabbi Yechezkiel Landau also served there for a time. There are two Yampol cemeteries. These were desecrated by the soldiers who threw the matzevot (headstones) into the River Goryn.

Thanks to the valiant efforts of a donor in New York, the cemeteries are being restored and a new Ohel (shelter) has been built over the graves of two of the rabbis (see pictures at the end of the book.) Workmen at the site, on their own initiative, rescued a number of the matzevot (headstones) from the river. See pictures from 2003 starting on page 159.

Notes to the Reader:

Within the text the reader will note *"[34]"* standing ahead of a page. This indicates that the material translated below was on page 34 of the original Yizkor Book written in Yiddish and Hebrew.

Monument to the Fallen

In memory of the dear and
beloved residents of YAMPOL
BELOGORSK and KORNITSA
brutally murdered by fascists on
27th June 1942.
You are in our hearts forever.

Survivors at Memorial

Family Notes

Yampol Yizkor Book

A City in Flames
Memorial Book of Yampol

(District of Volhyn)
(Yampol, Ukraine)
Latitude: 49°58' / Longitude: 26°15'

Translation of
Ayara be-lehavot; Pinkas Yampola, Pelekh Volyn
Edited by: L. Gellman
Published in Jerusalem, 1963

Acknowledgments
Translation Project Coordinator
Judy Wolkovitch

This is a translation from:
Ayara be-lehavot; Pinkas Yampola, Pelekh Volyn;

Town in flames; book of Yampola, district Wolyn,
Editor: L. Gellman, Jerusalem,

Commemoration Committee for the Town with the Assistance of
Yad Vashem and the World Jewish Congress, 1963
(Hebrew, Yiddish, 154 pages)

2   Yampol, Ukraine Yizkor Book

Table of Contents

Title	Author	Page
Translated from Hebrew		
A Memorial for Future Generations	Commemoration Committee for the Town	4
Judaism of the Heart and Mind	Arieh Leib Gellman	6
For Ukraine and its Towns	Y.L. Bieler	12
G-d of Revenge	Chaim Chemiel	13
About the Martyrs of our Times	Moshe Prager	15
The First Office of the Great Rabbi in Yampol, Yechezkel Landau	Arieh Leib Gellman	22
The Blood Libel Trial in Yampol Alarms and Horrifies the Jewish World	Professor M. Balaban	37
Tell me	Ezriel Goren	43
Tsaddikim and Hidden Tsaddikim in Yampol	Aharon HaLevi Pinchnik	50
Jewish Town	Judith Kleish	60
I Believe	Rabbi Shimon Effrati	60
Our Friendly Village, Yampol	Yaacov Horzshach	65
The First Yizkor of the Last Time	David Reuben	79
Reb Zalman the Poor (An Example of a Repentant Sinner in Yampol)	Dr Yitzhak Weisstaub	82
In Memoriam (A Lament for the Martyred Dead of Volhyn)	H.B. Ayalon	86
Extracts from the Ledger of the Chevra Kadisha of Yampol	Arieh Leib Gellman	90

Translated from Yiddish

A MEMORIAL FOR FUTURE GENERATIONS
[v]

Our town of Yampola, or, in the Russian pronunciation, Yampol, is considered to be one of the oldest communities in the region of Volhyn dating back to the expulsion of the Jews from Spain. (Researchers claim it was much earlier, around the 11th century.) When Jews were driven out from Spain, they spread out into different parts of Europe, attempting to find a temporary resting place in the Diaspora, yearning for a better future - the arrival of the Messiah.

We are dedicating the present volume to the memory of the people of our town, our relatives, friends and loved ones. They were decent, honest, innocent victims who were slaughtered in one single day, some of them even buried alive.

Yampol was built in a similar way to the other towns of Volhyn and for a few decades was static, with neither growth nor development. Most of the newcomers adapted to the new environment, making a bare living of frugality and poverty.

A few families left town in the last century, emigrating to the USA, Argentina and other countries. Only a few isolated families, such as Rabbi Shalom Yahalom and the rabbinical judge David (Rabbi Doodi) went to Palestine in their older days. A few of the young people arrived in Palestine 40 years ago and made a significant contribution to the rebuilding of the land and the establishment of the State of Israel.

Despite the town's stagnation economically and physically, Yampol did develop remarkably, both spiritually and culturally. Yampol produced scholars, intellectuals, chassidim and religious giants, who brought honor and esteem to Judaism.

This tranquil city, similar to other Jewish communities, shared the fate of other European Jews brought about by those evil enemies who shattered their roots, stems and branches. All of Yampol's Jews were exterminated without leaving even the tiniest remnant. The atrocities to which they were subjected struck them in the most severe, terrible ways.

The undersigned, who grew up and were educated in Yampol, who, thanks to the grace of G-d, escaped the terrible fate, were the sole survivors who escaped, some even before, and others after, the first World War. They now reside in Israel and felt a moral obligation to eternalize the memory of those martyrs whose entire lives were dedicated to noble and charitable activities. To our great distress we do not have pictures, documents or other records of the town during the last period, that of the Holocaust. We do not even have the date

{vi}

of the cruel slaughter. We know only one fact - the innocence, honesty, and righteousness of those who were killed and slaughtered. We hope the following articles will serve as a reminder of our loved ones, never to be forgotten.

COMMEMORATION COMMITTEE FOR THE TOWN
Arieh Leib ben Josef Gellman (Jerusalem)
Ezriel ben Baruch Goren (Pardess Hannah)
David ben Yitzchak Rubin (Kfar Chassidim)

JUDAISM OF THE HEART AND MIND
by Arieh Leib Gellman

[1]

The terrible suffering of the Jews, during the Holocaust, hit Yampol Jews hardest over the years 1943-1944. The incredible agony of millions of European Jews, unmatched in history, left deep wounds in the heart of Jewry. How could we ever forget the destruction of thousands of Jewish communities? Among them the community of Yampol, in the district of Volhyn, a community of people distinguished in their study of Torah, piety, intellect, ethics, morals and spiritual nobility. Their memory for us must be eternal!

The great trauma which that destruction caused to the Jewish people left its mark on the body and soul of the nation. Its heart is wounded, pained and depressed. A flame burns within us, a flame of hatred against the accursed murderers. Not only never to be extinguished, but increasing from year to year!. We cannot forget, we are not permitted to forget, it is impossible to forget!

The fortresses of Judaism, doomed to extinction, stand daily before our eyes. We can imagine the fire and sparks spread against Jews with unheard of venom. The millions of innocent souls who were thrown into flaming ovens by inhuman beasts of prey raise their voices to us, as do the sole survivors, demanding 'DO NOT FORGET'.

Their memory must be preserved by Jews all over the world.

The town of Yampol had a unique characteristic, different from its neighboring towns. Yampol belonged previously to the district of Kremenetz but during the Soviet occupation, it became part of the district of Shepetovka. According to the last census, it had more than 300 families. In Jewish records it became well-known because of the 'Blood Libel' of 1756.

The Jews of Yampol suffered a lot during the 'Libel'. Many were imprisoned and subjected to harsh interrogations. (The reader will find interesting details of this historic trial in the late Professor Meir Balaban's article in this volume). It is not difficult to imagine the hardships and tragedies of the townspeople as a result of this terrible libel. They also suffered much during the fighting between the Swedes and the Cossaks at the start of the 18th century. Nevertheless, "the Eternal [G-d] of Israel will not deceive" [I Samuel 15;29] and the town safely escaped from all harm and tragedy and continued to spin the thread of traditional life. The life of a quiet, folksy, chassidic, and enlightened town.

Despite the small number of Jews of Yampol, it was privileged to have some of the greatest Torah luminaries among its spiritual leaders, thanks to the many men of spirit in the town. Among the noted was the "Noda BiYehudah," Rabbi Yechezkel Landau. (A separate article can be found in this volume on the spiritual character of this genius whose fame spread throughout the Jewish world.) Furthermore, our town's leaders invited one of the famous students of the Ba'al Shem Tov, Rabbi Michael of Zloczow, as preacher, a post which he occupied for many, many years. He, as well as his son the pious Rabbi Yosef, are buried in the cemetery at Yampol.

For the main part, Yampol's Jews had limited means. They made a living from small trade or different handicrafts. Some had the good fortune to receive help from their relatives in America.

During World War I and the Russian Revolution, and shortly afterwards, the Jews of the Ukraine were subjected to many pogroms and sufferings which also hit Yampol's Jews. The soldiers of the Ukrainian, Russian and Polish armies plagued the Jews and stole their possessions. The pogrom of the Russian soldiers, headed by the fierce Hetman Shisko, brought desolation and destruction to the Jews of Yampol in 1919. Many were killed, many others wounded, and Jewish property was stolen. Matters improved, though only slightly, during the Communist regime. Some 20 years later, Yampol was occupied by the German army and the great glory of Yampol was extinguished forever.

A JEWRY OF HEART. This earnest title was bestowed by one of the Hebrew writers on the Jews of Volhyn. The Volhyn region did not glitter with famous scholars like Lithuania, but was noted for pure heart with simple folksy devotion to the underlying basis of a matter without paying attention to the superficial esthetics. It was mainly a Judaism of the heart and an outpouring of love and trust.

Yampol, however, differed from most the other towns of the Volhyn district. Not only did Yampol excel in matters of the heart and the spirit, it also had an intellectual Torah heritage, which was implanted in it by the outstanding pious, religious leaders who had been in their midst in previous generations.

The spirit of Torah and enlightenment was an integral part of Yampol Jewry, including not only scholars and intellectuals, but also the simplest artisans who gathered in the great synagogue. The town did not experience antagonism among its groups. Chassidim of Trisk, Zinkov and Ostra, lived in peace and harmony. The spirit of Enlightenment created some difficulty only for a few fanatics among the religious Jews, but they did not have a serious influence on the general populace. Typical is the fact that the Zionist movement and the political vision of Herzl made an impression among the Torah scholars, the enlightened and the simple folk. The fact that a small group of youths wrote a pamphlet by hand called "The Awakening" which spread rapidly among the readers of Hebrew symbolized the spirit of the cultural level prevailing in the town. The contributors to the paper were; Alter Rimel, Eisik Knif and Yaakov Horzshach of blessed memory, and the survivors David Rubin, Ezriel Goren and the editor of the present 'Memorial Book."

In numbers, there were only a few young men who devoted themselves entirely to Torah study, but in quality they rose to great heights. The elders of the town, among whom were accomplished scholars, discussed their study and scholarly novellae with these boys. It has been more than half a century since we parted from our dear town, but the image of these pious and noble individuals always pass through our mind. It is difficult to forget their knowledge in all areas of Torah study and their noble spirit.

A notable scholar was Rabbi Aryeh Leibish Lerner. He was one of the outstanding students of the famous Rabbi Shlomo Kluger from Brody. This was the second time that the leaders of the community went to Brody to choose a rabbi. The first rabbi was the world renowned scholar Rabbi Yechezkel Landau, author of "Noda BiYehuda" and other important Halachic works. Rabbi Leibish Lerner acted as local rabbi for over 60 years and passed away on the seventh day (Tishrei 7) of 5673 (1912). His son, Rabbi Meir Shmuel Lerner, followed his father and was highly respected by the Yampol Jews. He shared the fate of the innocent victims of the Holocaust and did not survive (HY'D). Rabbi Yosef Derbarimdiger, a descendent of the Berditshever Rav, Rabbi Levi Yitzak, served as a rabbinical judge at the time. He too perished during the Holocaust (HY'D).

The elderly Rabbi Aryeh Leibish Lerner (of blessed memory) was renowned in all the nearby towns as a halachic authority, and they all turned to him with their halachic questions. His custom was to come to the Kloiz early in the morning before dawn. He would then spend hours in contemplation. He was of much aid to the young scholars who studied in the Kloiz who turned to him for explanations of difficult passages in the Talmud. At an advanced age he became blind, but since he knew nearly the entire Talmud by heart, he still was able to reply immediately on important or minor matters without having to consult the Talmud. His erudition and outstanding memory were truly impressive.

Rabbi Eli Zeigermeister (Weisstaub), a frail short person, was an adroit scholar, "sinai" [=knowledgeable] and "oker harim" [lit. uprooter of mountains, i.e. a sophisticated analyst.] He studied and taught for many years, but never completed the entire Talmud because his analysis of each page of the Talmud took him several days. He wrote and published two books, "Minchas Marcheshes" and "Minchas

Machvas" which comprised commentaries on the Torah and analyses of difficult passages in the Talmud. He excelled by learning at a slow pace, but in depth; [unfortunately] he perished during the Holocaust, He wrote two essays, commentaries on the Bible and Talmud. The writer of these lines had the honor of assisting him in the preparation of the first volume which was printed in Berditshev. One of his sons, the late Dr. Yitzchak Weisstaub, was a student of Dr. Tzvi Peretz Chajoth, chief rabbi of Vienna, who helped him to enter the faculty of Medicine at the University of Vienna, and he became a physician. In his last years he joined relatives in Winnipeg, Canada, where he practiced medicine at the local hospital. As a writer, he was a frequent contributor to the weekly "Hamitzpa" which was published in Krakow. One of the essays he published is titled "The Poor Zalman of Yampol."

Rabbi Yisroel Feivishes was considered one of the greatest of scholars, and his influence on his students was tremendous. His specialty was the study of Halacha and rabbinical decisions. The author of these lines, one of his devoted students, studied with him not only the Talmud and Tosafoth, but also Shulchan Aruch Orach Chaim and Yoreh Deah (the laws of Kashruth). He personally knew the critic RIBA'L [Yitzchak Ber Levinson] but never spoke against him or criticized him in spite of RIBA'L's bitter opposition to Chassidism. He was careful to honor him as a great Talmudic scholar and analyst of Jewish thought. This demonstrates the patience and honorable relationship, which the orthodox had towards those who opposed their opinions and ideology in Judaism.

Rabbi Yankele Greidinger (HY'D) was a native of Yampol who had studied in our Kloiz and served as a rabbi in Greiding, in the district of Podolya. He was the only son of Reb Shimele. Once a year he would come to Yampol to fulfill the commandment of "Honor Thy Father and Mother" by visiting his parents. He took the opportunity to visit the Kloiz where he would join the students in their study. They would assault him with questions concerning the Talmud and Tosafoth. His explanations were excellent and wondrous, and were received by the youths with great pleasure.

Rabbi Yitzchak Meller from the nearby town of Lanivitz would occasionally visit our town. He was author of the well-known works "Ezra Lehavin", a wonderful super commentary on Ibn Ezra's bible commentary, and a unique pamphlet "Or Haganuz", a super commentary on "Or Hachaim". On his visits, he would spent time with the youths of the Kloiz, many of whom were already proficient in Talmudic and critical literature. This rabbi, who served afterwards as rabbi of several communities in Bessarabia, was also knowledgeable in secular studies, particularly mathematics and geometry. The youth of the Yampol kloiz were deeply influenced by his writings and enjoyed his visits immensely. The introduction to his book "Ezra Lehavin" as well as his last essay "Lehavin Imrei Bina" were important contributions to the field of critical literature.

In 1945, an emergency meeting of the Zionist Organization took place in London. The delegation of the Jewish community of Poland was led by a Mr. Sommerstein. A young grandson of Rabbi Meller, who during the Holocaust was a partisan, also attended the meeting. He reported the following: entering Yampol with his partisan group after the fall of the Germans, he found Yampol completely destroyed. The Ukrainian peasants from nearby villages told him that "all Yampol Jews were one day removed for burning and slaughter."

Rabbi Samuel Chaya's was a unique personage among the outstanding householders of the town. His house was always open for travelers or other Jews passing by Yampol. He was considered an accomplished scholar and his vast knowledge of Talmud was made available to students who constantly turned to him with every difficulty they found in any Talmudic passage. He was a friendly person, quiet and humble. He distanced himself from all local politics. His custom was to attend the last "minyan" of prayers each morning, and then he would spend his time with those young scholars who showed sparks of genius. They learned much from him and he is deserving of a blessing.

Rabbi Yankel Zalman's (HY'D) was the only "melamed" [teacher] who spread the study of grammar. In this subject he endowed his students with much linguistic and literary knowledge.

Thus the Kloiz produced young Talmudic scholars who were adept in the Hebrew language and literature. Worthy of mention are Reb Yitzchak Goldberg (known by the nom de plume "Itzi Moshe Hirsch's") and Reb Alter Rimel (know as "Alter Avrohom Elyakim's") who were among the first teachers to introduce the method of studying Hebrew in Hebrew (Ivrit b'Ivrit) in Berditshev, Ostra and other localities. Both were prolific gifted writers and occasionally published articles in the Hebrew and Yiddish newspapers. May their memory be blessed.

This little town raised and educated a Jewish intelligentsia, men of spirit, heart, emotion and wisdom, who in time developed and became writers and leaders in various lands who brought honor to the people and the state.

The holocaust and its destruction uprooted and eradicated from the world thousands of communities, but it did not succeed in extinguishing the holy fire, the sensitive feelings, and the noble spirit which they carried in their hearts up to the last moment.

The articles gathered in this volume are dedicated with admiration, deep sorrow and severe pain to the memory of our beloved townspeople, decent, faultless Jews, nearly two thousand, who marched erectly one Sabbath morning from their homes in to the death pits and ambushes of fire which the Nazis had prepared for them. They marched with dignity, vengefully despising their Satanic murderers who will be remembered as an eternal shame. Their names should be wiped from the face of the earth!.

May this Memorial Book serve as a monument to their pure souls. May the Almighty remember them beneficently among the righteous men of the world and may He revenge their innocent blood.

FOR UKRAINE AND ITS TOWNS
(A sound and lamentation)
by L. Bieler

[6]
My G-d, my G-d, my soul cries
Cry, daughter of Israel
Lament, and breathe
The fire consumed Israel

For the butchering of a people
Untold suffering, a waterfall of blood,
Old, young, no mercy
On the altar, an innocent sacrifice

For the babies, being nursed
Turn apart on the rocks
And for their blood which flowed
Right in front of their parents.
For destroyed communities
And for the catastrophe of the synagogues
Wood for fire
The beautiful cities of Israel.
For the generations who were cut down
Tears of fathers on tears of their children
In the valley of Auschwitz, they ended their lives
For the bonfires of the furnaces.
For the imprisoned, wearing sackcloth
Wiped out in the thousands
In Treblinka and Maydanek
There's no one to collect their bones.
For the trains full of people
Lined with plaster and sulfur
Dying of thirst, almost dead
Crying "water" and finding none.
For the girls who fainted
Wives who killed themselves
Ninety three pure ones died together
Their honor was protected.
For those who froze in snowy fields
Sweet children in their mothers' arms
And for the holy ones crying out
As they were buried alive in pits
For the desecrated parchments
In the hands of Nazis, enemies of G-d,

Ripped up, torn and defiled,
In the garbage and no one to rescue them.
For the saintly ones, the humble of the world,
Learners of Torah, the heads of the nation,
In the cells of poison their voices were choked.
The menorah fell, it was extinguished.
For the youth, the flowering of the nation
Fighting vanguards, lions of rebellion
Facing the criminals spilling blood
Burned in the flashes of fury.
For the rivers of blood and tears
A covenant of revenge in a heart is kept
In a ghetto battle unfading
Consumed was the strength of concealed heroism.
For the sanctification of G-d's and the nation's name
And for revenge for the blood of the pure
Ever stronger they gave up their lives
They fought, the heroes fell.
For the broken nation let us lament
Trapped with sorrow, wrapped by Holocaust
Will you forever hide hatred
And not bring out the shine?
See, G-d, my flesh is shriveled
My heart is broken, my enemies rise
Listen to my request, find a fast shelter
Save my soul from bloody men.
Rise hero, upon the dead
As a candle always shining and quivering
Every drop of blood a sacrifice to the devil
We shall always remember.

G-D OF REVENGE
by Chaim Chamiel

[9]
The oppressor was proud, and destroyed all that was dear
Destroyed, ruined, cut down and blown up.
Waves of hawks turned over cities
Homes - broken by tyrants
The Jewish Diaspora is filled with those hanged
And those who fell by the sword.
G-d! Have your mercies ended,
Or has the trait of Justice found another reason
Or praise for a Goy drumming at a dance of sacrifice
Inventing battles, churning new ideas?

Forget...and remember, until the very end of your cup I stopped finding
Send lightening and thunder! Pour on him your arrows of wrath!
Give your inferno and hell, your bitter destruction
Gather anger, take revenge, find my debt,
Enable me to grit my teeth for the dread in my heart
Strike him, shock him, with the shock of annihilation
Shatter him, break him into pieces before his master the Devil
Close the mouth of the "volcano" of this horror with great slap
For joy, contempt, and the spilled blood.
Take revenge, G-d, a revenge for the painful groans
The voice of blood cries out, with full heroism;
The heroes of Warsaw, Krakow and all the regions -
The holy ones of Volhynia, Podolya and the cities
To sanctify the name of your people who were mightier than lions
And defeated in their souls the disgusting monsters
The blood boiled, the corpses fell apart
And they cried out to heaven with the cries of wrath!
REVENGE!
Wail before your treasure, with noble lamentations
Pierced by lead, his body like a sieve
Those fainting gazed at a hard sky
And the path of the just followed them in blood...
G-d of revenge! If you hate an innocent child
And hid your face from a songful soul and innocent longings
Before you lock the gates of tears.
When people are beside themselves on the night of forgiveness
Holy ones were burned, the ruins rustled, the babies crushed.
They came to a small and stubborn people,
While speaking to you: "Since you are a G-d of pardon and mercy"!
They spilled tears, knocked on your gates
They raised their eyes to heaven, searched your face
They begged for their lives with sweat and trembling
Because they saw that their hands would not save them
They lit up their eyes in a flame.
Gather, G-d, their wrath and that of many others
They were slaughtered in public
And cast into pits;
The roar of the confused, the cries of the oppressed.
Tiny babies were sent to the slaughter,
He will combine, roar, bellow and make noise,
With powerful thunder, sulfur and fire.
Shock in detention the clucking of the viper,
The suffering of the shadow of death, give him generously,
Destroy his mischief, pluck out his eyes, kill him, annihilate him,
Let his daughters putrefy, his pregnant women be swallowed.

Wreck his blows, grind up his bones
Take revenge for an innocent girl, hanged on a rope.
Her braids were bloody with her neck and her scalp.
The curls of the girl, a crushed skull.
She gave up her soul with clear eyes
Burning and piercing...REVENGE!
Don't be still and don't hold back
Remember the child in school, who cuddled with you.
That in the merit of his sweet breath, the world exists -
Holding flames of the walls of the building.
Soldiers of annihilation and destruction surrounded him,
He escaped with "The Path Of The Just" in his hand,
And he sang the "Foundation of Chassidism and
Root of Divine Service" before the one G-d -
This is the song of freedom of a humming soul, longing for G-d.
The small one went into the fiery furnace in joy and happiness
He sang before his Creator, and made hearts tremble.
Their heart and soul sang to the living G-d
They sent machines of inferno, fire of destruction
Their souls left them in holiness and purity
Parchments of Torah were set on fire
And the flames consumed the walls of the house
To the sounds of calls of revenge, the song of the poet.
From your heights, G-d, scream like a woman giving birth!
Let not the blood be blood for your name
With spilled blood come and immerse your arm
And place it on the criminals who did not know your name
Terrify them and break them, because you are G-d.
Send your wrath, your inflamed consuming wrath
And burn them all up like on a bonfire
Until all sin is cleansed and purified
Until all evil and rebellion ends
So that all life will know
That the G-d of revenge has appeared!

ABOUT THE MARTYRS OF OUR TIMES
by Moshe Prager

[13]

Dedicated on Holocaust Memorial [Yahrzeit] Day, the tenth of Tevet, in memory of the millions of pure and holy souls, including more than 2000 of the people of Yampol who perished in 1943-1944 May G-d revenge their blood.

This is the story that has yet to be told - that of the martyrs of our times.

The period of the Jewish Holocaust in Europe revealed to us some majestic scenes of Jewish heroism. These inspiring images have already assumed an aura of legendary quality. We have the story of the fighters in the Warsaw Ghetto, the story of the partisans, the stories of escape and passage to Palestine. These stories were a significant source of inspiration for Israel's War of Independence. Yet this wonderful tale of modern martyrdom is still hidden, waiting for the dedicated historian who will collect the documents and testimonies and reveal the legendary splendor flowing from the facts.

"Where was your martyrdom?" I was asked recently by one of the leaders of modern Jewry. "The left wing circles, the socialists and communists, created the Jewish partisanka; the Halutz (pioneer) movement was prominent in the ghetto rebellion. But, what of Orthodox Jewry, or more accurately the millions of believing Jews? What was their response to the threat of genocide? We have not even heard of acts of heroism with religious zeal and martyrdom in the traditional religious sense of Kiddush Hashem [sanctification of G-d's name]. Since I have come to clear conclusions concerning this question after years of researching the period of the Holocaust, I answered as follows:

Admittedly, there have been very few reports of the many and varied manifestations of martyrdom in our time. On the other hand there are many accounts and indications of spiritual heroism and self sacrifice under indescribable conditions. So, the problem should not be put down to a scarcity of actual occurrences, but to a paucity of documentation.

With regard to the paucity of publications of this type of material, there are several reasons for this:

a) Very few of the elite of the religious Jewish community survived. The rabbis, heads of communities, leaders and religious activists and all those who served in religious roles in ten thousand communities spread over twenty one European countries that were occupied by the Nazi oppressor. They all perished together with their holy communities, and no one survived to tell the tale of their heroism during the years of dread of the Nazi regime, and of the fervor of the sanctification of G-d as they took their last steps. On the other hand, one should remember that the shining legend of the Warsaw uprising and of the deeds of the partisans came into being largely due to those who survived the camps. b) The few religious Jews who did survive are not keen to tell the tale of their survival. These are the very few elite who miraculously survived. A few admors [chassidic rebbes] and rabbis, yeshiva students, communal workers, members of the religious intelligentsia and others do not show any inclination to tell the story of their experiences and trials at the time when they faced the chasm of the abyss. This silence is typical. One must remember that this lofty experience of readiness to sanctify G-d's name, was a profound experience of consecration and elevation, literally as far as the very limits of the soul. Any one who went through this experience does not wish to describe it or glorify himself in it because they feel that the experience is profaned through its revelation. Moreover, these Jews who experienced the sternest spiritual test of all, do not consider themselves heroes at all. They humbly underplay their emotional experience of yesteryear: "What is there to tell? What did I do, and what is there to marvel at? Any Jew is capable of such behavior, because he is a Jew for this very reason!"...

c) There is no public institution involved in collating documentary evidence of acts of sanctification. For the very reason that the subject is very comprehensive and relevant to the experiences of millions of faithful Jews, there is no one to take responsibility for it. Unfortunately, a strange and shameful situation has arisen in the research of the Holocaust whereby each group chooses its own heroes from the six million victims. These heroes, all of whom are the 'private property' of each group, only they are worthy of a wreath of remembrance.

In an honest effort to reveal the historical truth, I recently conducted an educated attempt to research the subject of the sanctification of G-d's name only on the basis of evidence provided by non-religious and even anti-religious Jews. I am grateful to the Bund Archives in New York which granted me access to their large collection of Holocaust literature. I will attempt to present a concise summary of my findings.

THE AWAKENING OF FAITH

The first question:

What was the intensity of belief in the ghettos, torture camps and places where killing took place? Did people lose faith in the face of destruction? The Nazis waged a war of annihilation against the Jewish faith, methodically desecrated all things holy to Israel, and took every opportunity to abuse the G-d of Israel. How did this affect the repressed and humiliated Jews?

We were very surprised by the response:

Among millions of doomed people in the suffocating ghettos and the cramped conditions of the camps of destruction there were clear signs of a religious revival. Not only did the observant Jews withstand the cruel test and display boundless devotion to Jewish values, but there was a religious revival among Jews who were previously non-observant or even opposed to religion.

The following are descriptions and facts taken from different places and different circumstances:

The well-known poet: A. Sotskever, one of the leaders of the Jewish partisans, states in his book about the Vilna ghetto:

"The commander of the ghetto forbade praying or the holding of any religious ceremonies, but just as was with the conversos in the time of the Inquisition in Spain, the religious Jews did not abandon their faith. In Reb Shaulka's kloiz, a yeshiva was set up in the name of the late Rabbi Haim Ozer Grudzenski, attended by 30 students. Later, a yeshiva was established for small children. The yeshiva students studied at night, and during the day they were subjected to forced labor. Little was known in the ghetto about the two yeshivas."

Other chroniclers of ghetto life also talk of the revivalist movement and return to faith in the ghettos that were destroyed.

Religious feelings strengthened considerably in the ghetto. Jews assembled every day to pray. Even those who were thought of as secular came to pray with the minyans (based on 'The Remembrance Book of Breinsk,' published in New York in 1948.)

"Life in the town under Nazi rule changed things ... the number of observant Jews grew daily. People who had not prayed for many years became religious and prayed for hours on end and recited psalms. There were also instances of the reverse, but no one lost faith in the miracle that would surely come" (based on Yizkor Buch fun Rottne, published in Argentina in 1954.)

Another record of the events tells of the emotional traumas of the religious Jews. An eye witness of a public Nazi ceremony at which Torah scrolls were burned in the Galina ghetto, near Lvov, provides the following account (taken from the book 'The Scroll of Galina,' published in New York in 1950):

"The German officer gave the order to take all the Torah scrolls out and to burn them. At that moment the evil doers took the scrolls out, there were four or five of them, and threw them out near the synagogue. ... one of the Jews who were in hiding, Yerachmiel Wolf Khodak, ran out, fell at the Nazi's feet and begged him in tears to let him take the scrolls. "It's good you came here" shouted the German; "you will burn the 'Bible' yourself! Have you got any matches? Burn your 'Bible!' The Jew threw himself on the scrolls and replied: "Burn me with the scrolls! Even if you shoot me I will not carry out your order!" The murderer took out his gun, aimed it at the Jew and again ordered him to burn the Torah scrolls. The Jew jumped up, tore his shirt and exposed his chest to the murderer: 'Shoot! I won't carry out your order!'

"At the time, I was in hiding in the house of the Reb Abba'lle, the shoichet, together with his son-in-law, the Rabbi from Pruchnik. When we heard that the Torah scrolls were being burned we began crying bitterly with screams of pain. The Rabbi tore his clothes, fell to the ground and wept: "What is left of our lives? What are our lives worth now? We have been shamed! We have been shamed!" The people surrounding him tried to calm the Rabbi. He raised his head and lifted his eyes to the heavens and called out: "And we still have not forgotten Your holy name! We will continue to serve the blessed Lord!"

UNDERGROUND HOUSES OF PRAYER

The second question:

How did the Jews continue to conduct their religious life and traditions? In many places, the Nazis imposed the death penalty on anyone carrying out religious activities, for any assembly involving public prayer or for any one avoiding forced labor on the Jewish festivals. What did the Jews do? Did they observe the Jewish festivals? Did they organize underground houses of prayer? Did they, at least, take the risk of holding communal services on the High Holy Days?

Once again we were surprised:

The documents and papers in our possession show clearly that wherever they were, the Jews all tried to organize clandestine houses of prayer, despite the harsh conditions and the explicit death penalty carried by such activities. Special efforts were made on the New Year and Yom Kippur when crowds of Jews assembled for prayer, even in the concentration camps. Moreover, even in the camps of partisans who fought in the forests under Russian-Soviet command, Jews assembled to recite the Prayer of Remembrance.

It is worthwhile copying a few testimonies regarding the clandestine prayer assemblies which took place during the High Holy Days. It should be noted that all the records of life in the ghetto make little mention of these activities, as if it were a natural and everyday occurrence.

Here for example, is a description of life in the Polish town of Balakhtov:

"The torture which the Jews underwent during the High Holy Days was a particularly tragic event. Despite the ban on prayer assemblies, on pain of death, Jews gathered on these days, in groups and prayed with great fervor ... the Jews risked their lives, secretly removed the Torah scrolls from synagogues and hid them in different places ... in Pavianitska Street, two Jews were led away, cloaked in their prayer shawls and wearing their Kittels [white prayer gowns worn on Yom

Kippur], - they had been caught praying." (an extract from the book "Yizkor Bukh" published in Argentina in 1951.)

The same eye witness spoke of a Kol Nidre assembly which took place in the Majdanek concentration camp:

"I shall never forget the night of Yom Kippur and the prayer of Kol Nidrei in Majdanek ... it is impossible to describe the sorrow of the people who wanted to save their lives through praying to G-d. It was awesome ..."

The writer, Rebecca Kaviatkovska, wrote about the prayer assemblies in the Auschwitz concentration camp:

"The Jewish women from Hungary assembled and began praying. The Jewish women from Czechoslovakia and Poland followed suit loudly. In the face of death, the women forgave each other for any offense they may have committed, reconciled themselves and awaited the morrow with fear and trepidation." (Taken from the book 'Fun Lahger, Tzu Lahger,' published in Argentina, 1950.)

Rachel Auerbach tells of the secret spot for praying, and the El Malei Rachamim memorial prayers recited in the Treblinka destruction camp:

"And Tanhum also tells us about one youth - others also mention his name - who was called Meir Kapo. He was the son of a scribe (of Sifrei Torah, Tefillin and Mezuzoth) and had a good singing voice. He was very devout and every evening, after work, when everyone was shut up in the huts, he would stand up and recite the ma'ariv evening service and El Malei Rachamim, after which the Jews in the huts would loudly recite Kaddish ... the Germans loved to hear the Jewish religious songs (yiddishe schticklech), and until he was shot by the Germans he was honored by them as a "kapo" although he harmed no one." (Based on a report in the Warsaw communist newspaper 'Das Naye Leben.')

And the last and most important - the partisan's prayer in the forest: based on reliable evidence given by the leader of the Jewish partisans, the poet Shmerka Kachraginski:

"It was in 1943 at the beginning of the High Holy Days, the last remaining Jews in Vilna, despite the fact that most of them were not observant, felt a strong sense of longing for yesteryear which had ended so recently, for their observant parents, for their grandparents who had prayed. Even in the forest, they did not want to completely break away from the sanctified yesteryear, and they prepared to gather a minyan to pray under a makeshift shelter, to pour out the bitterness in their hearts to their Heavenly Father and to recite the

Remembrance of the Souls prayer." (Taken from a book entitled "I Was a Partisan" published around 1952 in Buenos Aires.)

ON THE LAST ROAD

The third question:

In their final hour, how did the Jews accept the death sentence, a fate of utter destruction? The merciless enemy declared incessantly that the Jews were being led to the gallows only because they were Jews - did not this arouse in the Jews a sense of Jewish pride, a recognition of Israelite martyrdom and of readiness to sacrifice their souls for the sanctification of G-d?

And at this juncture, we encounter a most surprising discovery:

It is true that, on their last road, many Jews felt a sense of Jewish pride and a recognition of having a mission, and being sound of mind and with clear convictions they took it upon themselves to sanctify G-d's name with their death.

These disclosures show just how wrong the hackneyed complaint against the martyrs is: "As sheep are led to the slaughter." Not at all! This was not a dumb, senseless and misunderstood act. In too many cases, this was a march to the Akeida (a willing sacrifice), out of pure faith and fervent devotion. Leading the march to the "(train) carriages of death" and towards the crematorium were the rabbis and community leaders. They ignited the sense of self-sacrifice in the people following them. They spoke words of farewell expounding on the great merit of martyrs.

This is an account of such a death march as recorded by one of the survivors of the Treblinka camp:

"In the train carriage, on the way to Treblinka, the mood is not bad ... people behave with dignity in life's final hours. An elderly man managed to bring his phylacteries with him and he was preparing to conduct his daily prayers before the Master of the Universe." (From "Podolyishe in Umkum" by M.Y.Feigenbaum, Munich 1948.)

Furthermore, there are some accounts in Holocaust documentary books. These are stories of an inner freedom espoused by our age's martyrs.

"The deportation was announced for the day after Yom Kippur ... On Yom Kippur, the Jews assembled at the Shtieblakh (small synagogues) to pray. It is difficult to describe or portray this prayer. Young people, who were far from religious life, pushed their way in, out of an inner feeling, and also came to pray ... maybe this is the last time, so we should be together with other Jews. The prayers were like confessions on the deathbed. That night, after the prayers, the Jews did not forget to drink l'chayim (to life), as was their custom. But this was the last time. The SS forces, Ukrainians and Lithuanians, were waiting to perpetrate their plan of murder ..." (From 'Yovel Buch, Gewedimet Di Kdoishim Fun Sokolow' New York, 1946.)

"At this time, as a group of elderly Jews was forced to sit down in the snow, all wrapped in their prayer shawls and prayer gowns (tallitot and kittels), waiting for death huddled together against the terrible cold. One old man, Reb Yitzchok Nochum Weintraub, took a bottle of spirits and a small glass out of his coat and offered drinks to his neighbors. The elderly people drank to each other l'chayim and to meet again in Heaven, and wished a bitter end to their murderers." (From 'The Destruction of Shedletz, Oif Di Churvois Fun Mein Heim' by Elimelekh Feinzilber, Tel Aviv1952.)

These accounts, faithfully quoted here without any interpretations, are just a sample of comprehensive and rich documentation. Unfortunately, there is no room to tell the tale of 'the other side' of martyrdom, i.e. self-sacrifice in saving other Jews and helping out brethren in distress. I would like to comment that here too, a completely erroneous concept has taken root. The lamentable phenomenon of the JudenRaten with the 'Jewish Police' should not conceal the heroic struggle of the extensive and long lasting self-help efforts in the ghettos. These activities were continued until the very end. When the documentary material on this topic is made available, we will know that it is not the dark characters of 'The House of Dolls' that represent the image of the Jew fighting for his soul.

THE FIRST OFFICE OF THE GREAT RABBI YECHEZKEL LANDAU IN YAMPOL
by Arieh Leib Gellman

[20]

A small town full of Torah Sages - Famed Tsaddikim found their place of rest there - The first settlers were exiles from Spain - He served there in the Rabbinate ten years - He accomplished much concerning spreading Torah study - He initiated many ordinances - The Ledger of the Chevra Kadisha was written in his own hand - Was involved in solving the problems of Abandoned Wives - A serious question from "Ashkenazic Scholars" - Accuses Rabbis who do not want to permit anything without payment.

(A)

The illustrious Rabbi, Yechezkel Segal Landau, author of the books: Noda BiYehuda (Famous in Judea), Tslach, Doresh LeZion (Seeker of Zion), Ahavat Zion (Love of Zion) and Dagul Merevava

(Outstanding Among Thousands), is known to the Jewish world as the Head of the Rabbinical Courts in Prague, an important city in the Jewish world, famous for its leading rabbis. Such leaders as the Maharal of Prague held office there and taught the Torah to the people. Unfortunately, although most of the chroniclers of Jewish history have told the history of Jewish life in many lands and portrayed life in the Jewish community, they did not give due attention to the spiritual greatness of the renowned rabbis and luminaries of Judaism of those eras, who occupied a leading role in the communal life and left their spiritual impression not only within their own localities, but rather spread their religious and ethical wings over the Jewish life far beyond the limits of their own communities.

The centuries following the 1492 Spanish Expulsion were rich in spiritual and religious life and as such are a distinct period in Jewish history. The great rabbis of these ages were not interested in matters of the community alone, but principally in disseminating Torah and in moral guidance. One of the towering Torah figures of his time was Rabbi Yechezkel Segal Landau (b. 18 Cheshvan 5474 [1714] in Apt; d. 17 Iyar 5553 [1793] in Prague) whose first appointment was at Yampol where he served for ten years. It was during this period that he first achieved fame through his deep Halachic responsa and his wonderful sermons. In a responsa (Noda BiYehuda Tinyana (vol. 2), Even HaEzer, Section 116), he writes to a rabbi on the issue of writing a bill of divorce (gittin), "In my first community they write "Yampola" (in Hebrew characters with an Aleph after the initial Yud). Were I the first to write a divorce contract (get) in that town, I would have written "Yampol" (without the Aleph), but since this was already the accepted custom when I arrived, I made no change.

Hebrew literature and particularly Ashkenazi literature, is full of biographical essays on Rabbi Landau, his nature, and his ideology as spiritual leader of Jewry during that period, but all of it centers on the Prague period. In order to complete the picture, a few of his Torah activities during the Yampol period should be added. My sources were his own writings, and reports I heard from the elders of Yampol, my birthplace. These stories were handed down father to son.

(B)

The town of Yampol, in the province of Volhyn, where I was born, educated and grew up, boasted, like many Pale or Settlement towns, a circle of leading householders. These included some Torah scholars, some well-educated in the 'enlightenment,' Chassidim, and pious men who would have been prominent even in a large city. Even though their livelihoods were irregular, and all struggled to make a living in the town or in the surrounding villages, an aura of nobility pervaded the town. Most of them had a good religious education, and even the simple people and artisans were drawn to the holy books. On Saturday and religious holidays, they would sit at tables in the study houses or kloizes, listening to Torah studies and sermons.

The town was near Kremenetz, Brody, Dubna, Ostra and Rovno, and came under their influence in Torah, Chassidut and general education. Yampol was the home and final resting place of the famous righteous men and fathers of Chassidut: Reb Yechiel Michel of Zloczow (d. 25 Elul 5546 (1786)); his son, Rabbi Yosef, known as the Righteous Reb Yossele of Yampol (d. 24 Tevet or Shevat 5572 (1811-1812). Rabbi Landau mentions him in Tslach (Tractate Beitzah, Chapter 1, page 5b), "Over forty years ago the brilliant Rabbi Yosef of Yampol asked ..." Besides his greatness in Torah and Chassidut, he was a religious philosopher and an expert on Maimonides' "Guide for the Perplexed," and other works. Some of the town's elders would tell of Reb Yitzchak Ber Lewinson (known by his Hebrew acronym: RIBA'L) author of Beth Jehudah, Teuda BeYisroel, Zerubavel, Efes Damim, and other works, who lived in Yampol for three years during the lifetime of Reb Yossele. He later moved to Kremenetz. It is well known that RIBA'L was a leading opponent to Chassidut. He visited Reb Yossele only once when he and a friend had difficulty understanding a passage in the 'Guide to the Perplexed'. Reb Yossele offered a satisfactory explanation, and RIBA'L said he regrets not having visited Reb Yossele before.

Other figures were Rabbi Yaacov-Yosef of Ostra, the grandson of Rabbi Yi'vi [abbreviation for Rabbi Yaakov-Yosef ben Yehuda] (d. 23 Tammuz 5609 (1849)); Rabbi Michele of Shomsk, grandson of Reb Michael of Zloczow, and other offspring of other Chassidic Rebbes.

This town was blessed with many famous Rabbis and Chassidic leaders during Chassidut's early years. Nevertheless, the town was free of the strife and controversy that were rife in other towns and communities when Chassidim first appeared.

This town, located on low ground between the hills (mountain ranges) surrounded by canals and lakes, existed in this manner for centuries. In the ancient cemetery, on the outskirts of the town, embedded in the ground, were old, worn-out tombstones, centuries old. Some called the town "the Miracle Sea" [Yam Pelle in Hebrew] on account of the many miracles that saved the townspeople from the periodic pogroms. It was commonly believed that the Jews had formerly lived in the hills, but were moved by the Gentiles to the lowlands so that if threatened, their only recourse would be to jump into the rivers ... So life flowed down the generations in that little town upon the Goryn river.

(C)

Who the early rabbis were who sat in judgment in this town, we do not know, just as we will never know for sure how Jews arrived here. (There is an old tradition that the original settlers were Spanish Jews who came here following the exile from Spain. Reb Yitzchak Ber Lewinson (RIBA'L) reports in his "Beth Judah" in 5517 (1757) an account of a great blood libel in the town of Yampol in Volhyn, "my great uncle, Rabbi Elyakim of Yampol, traveled to Rome at the behest of the great rabbis of the Four Lands who met in the Great Assembly in the town of Brody. He met with the High Priest (Pabst) (the Pope) to discuss the matter of the Blood Libel. He succeeded in bringing back an epistle to the entire kingdom of Poland, written in Latin signed in the Pope's own handwriting and sealed with his seal, to totally dismiss this empty Blood Libel. For six consecutive years the Rabbi was in Rome and he worked hard on this matter. He was highly respected by the Pope and his cardinals as a brave, intelligent man, well versed in the Torah. He was a descendant of Reb Yosef ben Shmuel HaLevi who was exiled by King Ferdinand of Spain." From this account we can conclude that the early settlers were Spanish exiles.

In 5505 (1745), Rabbi Yechezkel Landau, aged 30, was appointed Head of the Rabbinical Court of Yampol. Already at this young age, he was highly regarded by his peers and particularly by the famous Sages of the Kloiz of Brody, "who were lions and tigers in the Torah and in piety."

The fact that the townspeople turned to Brody, which was known for its Torah scholars, and chose the young Reb Yechezkel, about whom the great Kabbalist, Rabbi Haim Zanser, testified that "Yechezkel peered into Structure of the Chariot," [the reference is to the prophet Ezekiel's vision associated with the higher reaches of Kabbalah], is a testimony to the strong Torah character of the townspeople.

In the introduction "Words of Endearment" to the first volume of Rabbi Yechezkel Landau's classic, 'Noda BiYehuda' (Famous in Judea), his son, Rabbi Yakovka Segal Landau, a pillar of the Brody Jewish community, writes: "In his thirtieth year, the year of Tzaddik Be'emunatho [the righteous in his faith (Habakuk 2;4) 'Be'emunatho' has a numerical value of 505, to indicate the year he arrived in Yampol 5505] a divine wind bore him to my birthplace, Yampol. (On the outside of the eastern wall of the great synagogue in Yampol, which was twice destroyed by fire, the first time during the tenure of the Noda BiYehuda, was inscribed the date, *Ki mimcha hakol umiyadcha nathanu lach,* ["For all is from You and we have given from Your own hand" (Chron. I 29;14)] probably only some of the letters were meant to be counted since the total numerical value is 841. I was unable to determine the exact date - editor.) Like a lion he disseminated Torah to the public. Students began to flock to study with him. Every promising scholar who saw some success in his studies would come to him and 'dine' at his table. Thus the Jewish world was filled with spiritual leaders. Every day these young scholars would discuss his theories and recite his praises. They would tell of his intellectual power and of his high character. They spoke so highly of this great man that community leaders came to him for advice and he judged disputes within the community and his rulings were obeyed. Thus it was all the time that he was in this city, although it was a short time, he became the talisman of the town and did not think of leaving. His staff grew and blossomed throughout the area. The city was quiet during the ten years he lived in Yampol. But as soon as he left, the leaving of the righteous man left its mark, and the quiet did not last long. When he left he was joined by his son in law, my brother-in-law, the famed Rabbi Joseph, who was afterwards rabbi and rosh yeshiva of Posen. Our mother, the Rebbetzin, left with us the children the following summer and as soon as we had left there were bitter troubles [in the town] and we escaped with G-d's help. He had not yet reached his fortieth year in the year Chukath Hatorah ["the decree of the Torah" Chukath has a numerical value of 514 to indicate the year 5514] and he was appointed Head of the Rabbinical Courts and Rosh Yeshiva of the capital Prague. His place in Yampol has a special endearment, and its light and honor arrived at the beginning of the year Shira ["song" had a numerical value of 515 to indicate the year he left Yampol 5515.]"

(D)

In addition to his reputation as a scholar of great wisdom and stature in Halacha, Rabbi Landau was also a gifted speaker. As his son Rabbi Yakovka reports: "he suited every sermon to the occasion whether joyful or sad; he was highly praised by princes who had heard of his words and had them translated to their own tongue. Several of his translated sermons were printed."

During the Yampol period, Rabbi Landau concentrated solely on Torah analysis and Halacha study. From 5505 (1745) to 5513 (1753) he would speak twice a year, on Shabbos Hagadol (before Passover) and Shabbos Shuva (between Rosh Hashana and Yom Kippur) on complicated Talmudic passages. Thirteen of these sermons were collected in his book Doresh Zion on the following Talmudic passages:

1) Parshas Hamiluim - Rabbi Yochanan said Eliyahu will explain this in the future (Menachoth 45a)

2) Just as the [bitter] waters test her, so they test him (Sotah, beginning of chapter 5)

3) When the fourteenth [of Nissan] falls on the Sabbath (Pesachim 66a)

4) Akavia ben Mehalalel testified to four halachoth (Edioth chapter 5 Mishneh 6)

5) The men of Alexandria asked twelve questions of Rabbi Yehoshua ben Chanania (Nidda 69b)

6) Rabbi Yehudah ben Betheira testified to five halachoth (Edioth beginning of chapter 6)

7) Rabbi Abahu said `it is written "from the family of scribes etc."' (Shekalim chapter 5 Halacha 1)

8) Rabbi Chanina assistant to the Kohanim (Edioth Chapter 2 Mishah 1,2,3, Pesachim 14a)

9) The meal offering of the daughter of an Israelite who was married to a Kohen is burned (Sotah 23 in the Mishnah)

10) Rabbi Yosi ben Yoezer of Tsereda testified that Ayil Kamtsa (a variety of locust) is kosher (Edioth chapter 8 Mishnah 4, Pesachim 15a)

11) The four species of the Lulav, and the sermon begins with the Midrash Rabah Parshath Emor which explains the verse "There are three which were hidden from me, etc." [Proverbs 30,18]

12) Rabbi Yochana ben Gudgada testified that a deaf mute whose father arranged her marriage can be divorced (Gittin 35a)

13) and the greatest of all "Ya'al Kagam" [an abbreviation for six halachoth] (Kiddushin 521, Bava Kama 73a, Bava Metzia 22b, Sanhedrin 27a) divided into three sermons.

All these sermons discuss the most delicate Halachic issues and his mastery of all aspects of Torah was astounding.

It is interesting to note that all his books of sermons and novellae bear titles which include the name "Zion", "Doresh Zion", "Ahavat Zion", "Ziun LeNefesh Chaya".

In the introduction to his book, "Ziun leNefesh Chaya" [Monument for the Living] (known by the acronym "Tslach" this work comprises his novellae on the tractates of Brechoth, Beitzah, Pesachim), which includes both straightforward analysis of Talmudic passages and deep interpretations in Aggada (homilies), he explains why he gave the book that name:

"And Yechezkel said: 'What benefit will man see in his work, all his days of vanity' (Ecclesiastes 1,3; 6,12) if he does not leave a lasting memory after he is gone so that even beyond the grave, his lips will continue to speak clearly. So all my years, since I turned twenty, and G-d favored me with the opportunity to teach students, I have gained some noteworthy insights on several tractates of Talmud and the commentaries, and have pointed out observations which can arouse the interest of the students, but unfortunately I did not write them all down and unfortunately some have been lost. Now I must be content with that which I have written down. They appear here together with what my students recorded. Seven years ago G-d granted me the opportunity to publish my responsa "Noda BiYehuda" which I named after my father, and now I repay my debt to my modest and pious mother with this monument to her living (Chaya) soul. I have chosen this book on three tractates of the Talmud, Brachoth, Pesachim, Beitzah, A Monument for the Living Soul ... I called my responsa Noda BiYehuda after my father [Yehuda] ... and I have called this volume Ziun Lenefesh Chaya "a memorial (Tsiun) for the soul of the living (Chaya) in honor of my mother, Chaya."

"I must point out that all my insights are for the benefit of students; the great Torah scholars can do much better. I prepared a pauper's offering. Nevertheless, even greater men than myself may benefit from this book, if only that it will save them time. Thoughts that took me several hours of work to reach, will be immediately accessible to them. A particularly difficult subject was the passage of Rabbi Chanina S'gan Hakohanim (Pesachim 14a), which afforded many a sleepless night. Especially Maimonides' interpretation of this passage in his introduction to Tahroth, one of the orders of the Mishna, was very puzzling until, with G-d's help, I succeeded in resolving it. I now offer thanks to G-d for the fifty years He has enabled me to teach Torah. I pray that I will live out my days in such a manner and that He will enlighten me and my children and students in the light of the true Torah."

(E)

The elder Torah scholars in our town liked to talk about that great era; about the yeshiva that Rabbi Yechezkel maintained in his study house, and his method of teaching Torah. One of the older men would point to his seat in the study house. Such was the oral tradition he had heard. As an indication of the power these memories had for the scholarly crowd (which even in my day was dwindling,) is the existence of two closed bookcases, which were kept locked. These bookcases housed the study books that had served the students in that golden era. As one of the regular students at the study house, I was once allowed by the sexton to examine the contents of the bookcases. There I found some Talmud tractates, Rav Alfas, books of morals and some Halacha books, etc.

Decades had passed since Rabbi Landau's office in Yampol, yet his influence was still felt in the curriculum of the schools and adult study groups. His method is well known as it was laid out in his books. He strongly objected to empty intellectual acrobatics and he demanded that all discussion be directed toward determining the Halachic ruling. This method was adopted not only in Yampol but in all of Volhyn and the surrounding districts.

Rabbi Yechezkel's second son, Rabbi Shmuel Landau, who succeeded him in Prague explains his father's system in his introduction to 'Doresh Zion.' "The great and straightforward men devote their principal energies to extracting the Halacha from each topic and to resolve apparent contradictions. Even correct analyses and differentiations, which can enlighten the students in the correct methods of study, are proper to raise," but not "empty sophistry which you may turn over and over and still remain with nothing worthwhile. Rabbi Horowitz (the Shelah) has already castigated those who study in this manner. They are in the category of `those who reveal false faces of the Torah. Their conclusions are based on weak and scanty evidence and their efforts are wasted. They are drawn away from the true path and use their intellect to develop incorrect ideas and at the end of the day they remain empty of Torah and do not arrive at a Halachic conclusion...."

Thorough investigation into the Talmudic sources and Halacha rules, in order to discover the Halachic ruling, - this was his method. Although all the paths of Aggada, the Zohar and Kabbalah were clear to him, he nevertheless refrained from writing on these matters. In his "Tslach [Ziun Lenefesh Chaya] on Berachoth page 33 he writes: "It is true that all our Rabbis' writings in Aggada are in code and riddles. Those who are capable will grasp their meaning, each scholar according to his level. My own feeling is that the revealed Torah was handed down to us and our children on Mount Sinai, but the hidden Torah was only hinted at, and even this only in part. But we hope that G-d will reveal His Presence before us once again and then He will reveal the hidden depths of the Torah's secrets as He did previously on Sinai."

In a Responsum sent to the Ga'on Rabbi Yeshaya Berlin (Yoreh Dei'ah 2:161) who wondered in his question why he does not respond in relation to Aggadic (homiletic) matters he replies:

"...Behold, I am surprised - what is the point of going on at length? Do the words of our Sages, then, require approval? Is there anyone foolish enough to darken the great light, to ascribe error to words of Aggadah? All the words of the masters of the Talmud, without exception, were "given by the One Shepherd," and they do not contain anything which is empty or untrue. If anything appears empty, it is our fault, and a consequence of our lack of intelligence, and the weakness of our ability to clearly comprehend the deeper allusions of their words.

Of course, if a person has the spare time, he should try his best to probe the meaning of words of Aggadah as well. All I said was that it is not my custom to reply to inquirers on such matters, because all the words of our Sages in Aggadic matters are sealed and closed, and they are all difficult to understand (at first sight), and if we start trying to explain them, there is not end to the matter, especially for someone like myself, who is burdened by public duties - it is enough for me if I find the time to reply on practical issues."

There is nothing which stands in the way of Halachah. This was his fixed and clearly-paved path, in which he guided thousands of students, who spread the teachings of their teacher throughout the Jewish Diaspora.

(F)

In the decades during which Rabbi Yechezkel lived in Yampol, he worked and achieved a great deal to spread the study of Torah, and he continued this holy task with greater energy and greater dedication in Prague, until the day of his death. In his Responsa he always excused himself for the delay in his replies, as a result of his constant distractions due to his students, whom he loved and cherished with all his heart and soul.

His timetable was such that he used to deliver four lectures every day, and on Fridays he would study with his students Chumash with the commentary of Rashi (he had a particular inclination towards the study of Rashi, because he held that he was himself a descendent of Rashi.) In a Responsum to one of his disciples he writes (Even Ha'ezer 1:56): "I received your letter, and I remembered how you used to stand before me in the community of Yampol, and your devotion to Torah, and I was pleased that you have achieved the status of being a true teacher to the community of the Lord. As for your complaint that you wrote to me twice, and that I have refrained from replying to you - this is not my custom to any learned man, let alone in relation to my student whom I reared and nurtured."

Apart from the burden of the Yeshivah, which was placed upon him, he enacted various ordinances relating to affairs of the town, and he instituted order in the conduct of the Chevra Kadisha (Burial Society.) The ordinances in the Register of the Chevra (which will be reproduced at the end of this book) were written in his own handwriting. I myself have looked through this Register many times, and I was astonished by his perfect handwriting, which was clear and free of corrections. The Register was copied out for me by the local rabbi, Rabbi Meir Shmuel Lerner, the son of the old rabbi, the Ga'on Rabbi Aryeh Leibush Lerner, who was the principal disciple of the Ga'on Rabbi Shlomo Kluger of Brody. The Ga'on Rabbi Aryeh Leibush Lerner served as Rabbi of Yampol for more than sixty years. The contents of the Register are similar to those of all such Registers, which record the ordinances of the Chevra and its decisions. Even though they have no particular historical importance as such, it is worthwhile saving them from oblivion, since they were written by the hand of one of the greatest of Rabbis, whose everyday conversation was imbued with holiness.

Apart from the ordinances in the Register, various other ordinances are mentioned in his work 'Noda BiYehudah.' In Orach Chayim 1 ch. 33 we find an ordinance concerning the lighting of candles by a non-Jew on Yom Kippur. He replied to the inquirer as follows: "Concerning your astonishment, that many communities have the custom that a non-Jew lights candles on Yom Kippur at the time of the Ne'ilah service - you should know that here in our community this custom has already been stopped, thank G-d, and also when I was in the community of Yampol, when I arrived there I found that this was their wont and I stopped it. However, I did allow a non-Jew to move the candles which had been lit before Yom Kippur, and to spread them out throughout the synagogue, and this is permitted because it is a rabbinic prohibition applied to another rabbinic prohibition [i.e. doubly light in severity] which occurs at the time of performing a mitzvah.

Another ordinance which he established relates to the chalitzah shoe [*1]. In his Responsum (what is a ... (Ever Ha-ezer 2:154) he writes: "When I came here (to Prague) I discovered that their chalitzah shoe was cut at the back out of three pieces, and I changed it to two pieces. And when I first came to the community of Yampol, I also found that they had a shoe made of three pieces, and I did not want to change it then, and I allowed it for a number of years until I saw the work Yamshed Shelomo on Tractate Yevamot, in chapter 12 paragraph 7, and I said it is sufficient to reduce the number of pieces and not to add a third one for no reason. There is no doubt that the more pieces you have, the more there is a problem of 'patchwork' shoes, especially since the third piece is superfluous and unnecessary. As far as winding the straps is concerned, the custom is to start from the front towards the back, and one starts winding it round behind the foot.

In the previously-mentioned Responsum regarding lighting candles on Yom Kippur, we see a glimpse of his powerful personality as a leading and decisive halachic authority. Which rabbi nowadays, however well-known, would dare to say publicly (Orach Chayim, ibid) "Who asked the community to do this, to recite piyutim (additional liturgical phrases on festivals)? Let them not say piyutim and selichot, but rather, listen to the cantor, and not do something which is forbidden according to the opinion of most authorities." The Noda BiYehuda was not afraid or intimidated, but rather, decided what he felt to be correct according to his understanding of Torah. Many of his rulings occasioned storms from time to time, and considerable disquiet in Rabbinic circles, but he, as a person who was firm in his views, took no account of his opponents and antagonists, since only the truth was his guiding light.

(G)

As soon as he arrived in Yampol, he became involved in a complicated problem, which required considerable research and a capacity for bold ruling. We find his Responsum about this in Noda BiYehudah (Choshen Mishpat 1:7) written "halfway through the month of Tammuz 5505 (1745) in Yampol."

"It happened in our community that the deceased Reb Segal passed away to eternal life. Reb Aharon then produced a document signed by the deceased in the sum of 10,000 coins by way of capital, apart from profits. The heirs argued that, on the contrary, it is he who owed our father money, because we heard our father complaining vociferously that he did not know what to do about Reb Aharon, "in whose hands my money has been lying idle for a considerable time and which I cannot recover." Now in the estate of the deceased we find two blank signatures of the above-mentioned Reb Aharon, and we have to settle this matter, because it seems to me that there are a number of uncertainties here."

After clarifying the issue from all possible angles, he ruled that "We have to speak up on behalf of the orphans, and allege that their father had paid off his debts, even though he left the document in the hands of Reb Aharon, because he could have employed various stratagems to avoid liability. For example, he could have written out a deed for the stipulated amount. Therefore he did not bother to recover his deed, because this stratagem is better than selling all his property."

Here we see the Noda BiYehudah sitting in his "Torah laboratory" dipping his hands deeply into the murky world of the halachic queries which engulfed the Jewish world of his time. He goes from strength to strength, from monetary matters to questions of life and death. He deals with questions of agunot [abandoned wives,] or, as he himself puts it in one of his Responsa "to save Jewish women from the chains of being an agunah." Anyone who studies this section of his Responsa (Even Ha'Ezer chapters 312 - 315 etc.) dealing with a discerning eye, cannot but be impressed and moved by the brilliance of mind with which he was blessed.

In these Responsa - which are his first decisions and rulings - we see the power of his genius, penetrating to the depth and breadth (of a subject), drawing from ancient sources, analyzing with subtle logic the relevant issues, and reaching a conclusion - of a lenient nature. He constantly emphasizes that he is one of those people who are "hesitant to rule," and in one Responsum (Even Ha'Ezer 1:32) he writes "I am one of those who are afraid to rule because I know the weakness of my abilities, lacking as I am in the power of a man, and especially in relation to a serious issue such as a marital problem, to untie and break the chains of a 'tied woman' - and this is something which should be placed on the table of princes - by which I mean Rabbis - who are familiar with the whole of the Talmud, from whose attention nothing escapes, and should not be asked of someone of such lowly status as myself (for what place is there for stubble together with pure wheat?) - but what option do I have, since the matter is one which has occurred within my sphere of jurisdiction, and I am therefore obliged to deal with it in the first place, to take pity on the misfortune of this poor woman and to heal her wounds."

Despite this, we find another contemporaneous Responsum of his (Even Ha'Ezer 2:128) where he stands firm in his approach, and writes "The conclusion relating to this woman is that if my permissive ruling was written before you, Sir, ruled in the negative, I stand firm by my opinion that she is permitted, and just as I ruled then, so do I rule now, with the power of leniency."

And the greatness of this giant of spirit reached such great heights that he could retract his previous opinion and admit "I was wrong." In one of his Responsa (Even Ha:ezer 1:28) he adds in a footnote: "Says Yechezkel - this responsum I wrote whilst yet a child, about thirty six years ago and because I was very young, I was exceedingly fearful of taking decisions and I tended to strictness in most of my reasoning rather than to leniency ... but now I have changed my mind and that which I said (then) is in fact mistaken."

Commensurate with his greatness is the degree of his humility. Nothwithstanding his great power of decisiveness, there are occasions when he stipulates in advance (ibid. chapter 29 towards the end) "that you should not rely upon me at all, unless you obtain the agreement of three leading authorities ... If they bestow their approval on my words and agree to permit it ... then I too will join 'the lions' since I am sure that their intention is for the sake of Heaven and that if they rule leniently, it is not because of any desire to benefit financially ... but in any event, they should not base anything they say upon me because it is possible that I have missed even a simple thing, which is not radical in any way, but rather, the great authorities of this generation should put forward their proofs and justify their positions as against me, for if

I do not possess seniority (in age) how can I possess wisdom? And I am, after all, but an empty vessel, a new vessel, if it pleases them."

(H)

Amongst the other difficult queries - perhaps the most difficult - which came before him when he first lived in Brody, and then in Yampol, was the following question, one which caused him (according to the testimony of his biographers) much anguish and soul-searching.

In the year 1744 he received a query from 'Ashkenazi scholars' of a certain community, whose name is not mentioned in his lengthy Responsum (Even Ha:ezer 1:72) so as not to upset the family concerned, which was a distinguished and respected family. Furthermore the father of the husband was a powerful man, who made use of civil law courts, and who had obtained from the judge a harsh ruling to punish severely anyone who would publicize the matter.

The facts of the case were as follows. Serious rumors had been spread about the woman who was the subject matter of the query, to the effect that she was an immoral woman. In that town there was a custom "that before Rosh Hashanah ... a number of.people would come before the Beth Din .. to confess their sins and to receive some.sort of penitence, as would be determined by the spiritual leaders, by way of fasting or deprivation, each one as appropriate to the extent of his iniquities and each one would come by himself."

As a result of their confessions, it became known to the Beth Din that the woman concerned was guilty of immorality. The rumors increased on a number of occasions but because the woman's family and that of her father-in-law, were powerful people given to violence, they managed to hush them up. But now that the Beth Din saw that a number of men had been ensnared in the trap of this adulterous woman, they came to the decision to inform her husband's father one night, in a gentle fashion, and with the exercise of a degree of discretion, seeing that he was such a powerful and forceful person.

After some days had passed, the husband's father came to the Dayanim and asked them to send one night for the penitent confessors and to cross-examine them, after application of the threat of excommunication (if they were to tell a lie.) The Dayanim did indeed do so that very night, and having been warned about the excommunication, they said what they had to say and they told the husband's father that night. Immediately he threatened that he would reveal the names of the witnesses and he gave instructions to beat them up cruelly but they refused to tell him the names and they said to him quite reasonably, "Why do you want to have a adulterous woman in your house?"

The responsum continues with a detailed account of the inquiries and investigations and the testimony presented before the Beth Din, "and afterwards the relatives of the woman spread a rumor that the witnesses were suspect and disqualified to act as witnesses." After exhaustive investigation, the Dayanim came to the conclusion that this rumor was groundless and they could not be disqualified." And then the father of.the husband went to the civil courts, together with the wife's relatives, to lodge a complaint against the Dayanim and witnesses, and the ruler became very angry with them and imposed a severe punishment on them, both physically and financially, and he ruled - on pain of a large fine which would be impossible to pay - that no one should say anything about this matter. In short, the husband's father carried out the threat he had made at the beginning. "And now the husband and wife want to continue living with one another - and we request a ruling as to their status according to the laws of.our holy Torah."

[From the sermon which he preached in Yampol on Shabbat Shuvah in the year 1753 (see Doresh Letziyon, Derush 13) we learn that this difficult query came to him whilst he was still in Brody in 1744, as he writes "And behold, approximately nine years ago I gave an answer to this difficulty - noted by the son of the author: See Noda BiYehuda 1 Even Ha-ezer 72 and 74, and Noda BiYehuda 2, Even Ha-Ezer 77 at end."]

The woman concerned was a native of Yampol but when the Noda BiYehuda received the query "from Ashkenazic sages" of a certain community (whose names are not mentioned, for the reason given previously) he was not intimidated nor cowed by the potentially serious consequences. He began to analyze the question with reasoning of astonishing brilliance and scholarship. And after clarifying - on the basis of sources in the Talmud and halachic authorities, whether early or late - all the possible arguments one could find to absolve the woman, he concludes by way of practical ruling "that this wife is forbidden to her husband by means of a severe prohibition of Torah law and she is considered "impure" (forbidden) just as any incestuous relationship and if her husband does not divorce her, then he too is not free of guilt, and he shall bear the consequences of his iniquity and the rest of the Jewish community is blameless."

The scholars of the "kloiz" in Brody, including the Ga'on Rabbi Meir Margolioth - author of the work "Meir Nesivim" and amongst the greatest scholars of that time - the Kabbalist Rabbi Chaim of Sanz, the well-known Chassid Rabbi Avraham Gershon Kaitover (brother-in-law of the Ba'al Shem Tov) and others, supported the ruling of Rabbi Yechezkel. They were very incensed over the perversion of justice and audacity of the wealthy men, in particular, the father of the husband, who was - as previously noted - a powerful man who utilized all resources, based on the judgment in the civil courts, to ensure that the ruling should not be publicized anywhere. Similarly the family in Yampol could not forgive Rabbi Yechezkel for this ruling of his and became his enemies for as long as he lived in Yampol.

Dr. Klein, who was one of his biographers, and wrote about him in a German anthology, speculates that he was forced ultimately to give up his post in Yampol because of this ruling of his. It seems to me, however, that this is an unfounded speculation. What is most surprising is that some of the elders of the town, who were very familiar, by way of traditions from their parents, with many details of his public life, do not mention this episode at all and never suggested that it was because of this that he had to seek a new post. The reason why he chose to move to Prague is very simple: because he was too restricted in a small town.

(I)

Before he left Yampol in July 1755, he responded to a difficult question (Even Ha'Ezer 1:36.) "A certain person went on a journey from the community of Brailov to "little Poland" and did not return home. After making inquiries, they found the corpse of a dead man who had certain identification marks on his clothes and body. His wife said that her husband had an identifying mark, namely a scar from a wound he had had on the finger next to his right index finger but on the corpse they found there was no such scar, although there was a scar on the finger next to his left index finger. The grandfather of the woman, who presented the query to me, said that it is quite likely that she made a mistake and that she made a slip of the tongue between "right" and "left" and they should therefore question her again."

In his reply he excuses himself on the ground that he was about to leave the town and that he had no books with him because many of his books had been burnt "because we had a great fire in our community and those books which I saved from the fire I have already sent on ahead. I do not have any place of rest so how can I respond to such a serious query without research [in my books?] But our generation is an impoverished generation and there are some people who are familiar with the words of the halachic authorities but do not want to give a permissive ruling unless they gain financially thereby and they take bribes to issue decision. There are others who wish to be considered wise and are not familiar with halachic authorities. And so I said [to myself]: Come what may, 'let me turn aside for a while and have a look' and maybe I can find a solution for her, especially as I declare that no one should rely on my decision alone until it is supported by leading halachic authorities."

And after clarifying the problem at great length, starting with the early sources, from the Rif and Rambam, until the most recent contemporaries, "and the principal authority on this is the Ga'on Maharal of Prague" he concludes by ruling "that we can put together various grounds for leniency and permit this woman, based on the various marks of identification, including the clothes ... with a clearly stated proviso, however, that two leading halachic authorities agree with me ... and if they agree with me - well and good, but if not - everything I have said is null and void because I have already written that my books are not here and I am writing in a hurry as I am going to be leaving here, the holy community of Yampol, within the next few days ... on Monday, the 6th of Av 1745."

In this Responsum the Noda BiYehuda spreads a clear light about the sorry state of affairs which then existed in a number of communities in the Rabbinic world. The clear accusation against certain Rabbis of that generation "that they do not want to permit anything without financial gain and they take bribes to judge" is a heavy accusation which only a Torah giant such as he could permit himself to make and this was typical of the strength of his Rabbinic personality.

THE BLOOD LIBEL TRIAL IN YAMPOL ALARMS AND HORRIFIES THE JEWISH WORLD
by Professor M. Balaban
(Of Blessed Memory)

[34]

The Bishop Anthony Kobilsky (an anti-Semite) died in January 1755. His successor to the diocese of Luck-Brisk was his sister's son Anthony Arazem Volovitch, who was also secretary to the Queen Maria Josepha, the wife of Augustus III. He exceeded his uncle in his hatred toward the Jews, and in this diocese he brought them to the level of oppression. Very soon afterwards there arose the matter of the trial in Yampol near Kremenetz because of which the entire Jewish community was imprisoned.

In Yampol, located in Volhyn district, close to Kremenetz, the corpse of a well known drunk was found near the Horin River on the Christian Great Sabbath [Easter Sunday] that fell on the 4th day of the Jewish Passover in 1756. The monks jumped at that find, but the Jews preceded them and asked a recognized doctor to examine the corpse. It was clarified that the corpse didn't have any wounds. The Jesuits decided to bury it far away from the city, but before they finished the burial there came a group of monks that took back the corpse to one of the churches in the city. The Jews, who carefully followed all that was going on, had the feeling that the monks were too involved with the corpse. Indeed, while on the way to the church the mob started claiming that the poor drunk's corpse was full of bleeding wounds and blows. The Jews demanded again a doctor's examination of the corpse, and with the report they stood in front of the judge in Kremenetz. The judge didn't believe the mob and the Jews of Yampol were released and the body returned for burial.

But the mob in Yampol did not give up and immediately filed a request with the Graf, Michael Kozimizh Radzivill, concerning a second inquiry into the same matter. Radzivill accepted the request but again the judges acquitted the Jews. The Christians still did not give up and referred the matter to Bishop Volovitch who demanded a third trial from Radzivill, and when the latter attempted to refuse, Volovitch threatened him with the interdiction of the church. Radzivill gave in and gave permission for a third trial on the same charge, first appointing three noble judges. These were replaced by three priests who were appointed by the Bishop and the accused were tortured. No one admitted anything in spite of the fact that they were tortured with such cruelty that two of them fell down dead in the hands of the hangman. Tortured and burnt by fire and by red hot iron, the Jews were returned to their homes to recover, but soon afterwards they were taken and were imprisoned in a dungeon located under the Graf's palace.

The news spread like wildfire throughout the whole country. The Rabbi of Biala wrote to Rabbi Yaakov Emden regarding this matter, also describing the turmoil that occurred at the Council of the Four Lands that had convened during July, August and September in Konstantinov. "I was" he writes "in the holy community Konstantinov for two weeks... There was there a deep impression as a result of the Blood Libel in connection with the Jews of Yampol who had been trapped in an evil plot much like the libel which had occurred in Fabiltsh (Zitomir.) All the prominent Jews were taken in iron chains."

One of these prominent community leaders, Rabbi Elyakim, son of Rabbi Asher Zelig, succeeded, while risking his life, in escaping from the jail in Kremenetz (where the trial took place.) He came in front of the same council in Konstantinov in tears to tell of the bad things happening to him and his brethren. The mood of the council at that time was not very sympathetic regarding this matter. The council was taking care of another disaster that could have hurt the whole Jewish world. At this time the events in Podolya had threatened to cause a split in all of Polish Jewry. [The entire region, which was later known as the Pale of Settlement, was under the control of Poland.] There had appeared that infamous seducer and instigator, Yaakov Frank, and there also he broke the Jewish laws and restrictions which had been recently dealt with by the rabbinical court [of the Council] in Brody in 1752.

Rabbi Emden writes about this in his book: "How long will such evil be carried on by the priests of Poland (a land of great darkness,) priests who are thirsty for blood like wolves and many a time shed the blood of poor and innocent people, like they had done the previous year when they murdered several holy souls for no crime on their hands? Land, do not cover their blood! [Job 16,18] The vengeful G-d avenges the blood of His servants and brings vengeance upon His enemies [Deut.32,43], smashing His enemies heads [Psalms 110,6] for on the same day three of the greatest tyrants suddenly died: - the Priest of Yampol, the instigator who demanded the shedding of innocent blood and the judge of Kremenetz where the trial was held."

The Gathering of the Council of the Four Lands on the Matter of the Blood Libel in Yampol

At the gathering of the Council of the Four Lands in the month of Elul, in 5516 [1755] in the city Konstantinov, many currently pressing matters were discussed. Primarily the great danger and the double-edged sword that was held over the Jews by the wicked followers of Shabbatai Zvi, may his name be blotted out, and his successor, the seducer and instigator, Yaakov Frank, who wandered in from Turkey. This accursed sect did great damage to the Jews who were attracted to it by their lies and false statements that were liable to destroy the entire Jewish world.

In the meantime there was nothing to be done except to confirm and strengthen the ban that had already been declared in various communities and had been repeated several times at the time of new moons and fasts of Monday, Thursday, and Monday, with blowing of the Shofar and extinguishing candles and other similar means. And like a thunder on a clear day there fell upon this gathering the distressing announcement of the Blood Libel in Yampol, an announcement that upset and perturbed the delegates and the Rabbis. One of the Yampol residents, Rabbi Elyakim, the son of Rabbi Asher Zelig, appeared with tearful eyes before the participants and told them about the terrible bloody proceedings of the trial that was taking place in Yampol. This is the way he described these most awful moments of his life: "Fifteen souls, the prominent leaders of our community, were caught unfortunately and suffered great bitter tortures and they are still in prison. Who can account for the great expense that it had cost to prevent even more from being arrested? There is already a big deficit, and we are completely impoverished. And here am I, one of those whom they schemed to kill, and only by the grace of heaven I escaped with my life; they looted all I had and all I have left is my soul. When I left the city I raised my eyes in prayer saying: Show me, G-d, your way! At this time the meeting time of the "shepherds" came up, the gathering of all the leaders, the patrons, and the community officers as well as the Rabbis our luminaries, of the Four Lands of our country Poland, and I said: 'I'll go there with a great noise to find some solution. Is it our destiny to die, G-d forbid?' With G-d's help my idea came to fruition. After we had discussed all aspects of the problem we concluded that the way to bring light among the Jews in their places of exile is to go to the city of Rome to request of their high priest, their mighty ruler, the beneficent Pope and the other Christian wise men who sit in their ruling council to issue a decree to all the governors, the priests and the judges not to listen to the lies and nonsense, that the intellect and common sense deny, and to declare that all the witnesses are lying since they are paid by Jew baiters. All the delegates looked at me, because it was my individual obligation to take my part in the distress of Israel... and I myself felt obligated in this matter and I therefore vowed at the time of my distress to go to Rome and with G-d's help, I arrived home safely ...."

Thus there was no other way but to journey to Rome, to the Pope, and plead in front of him to give them a letter stating that the church is against the Blood Libel connected with the Jews. There were more than a few of these letters at large although not a single one was ever published in the official "Biliarom Romanum."

After the terrible trial in Fulde in 1235, Pope Innocent the Fourth published four letters between 1235 and 1247, one after the other, all concerning the same matter. A similar letter was written also by Pope Paul the Third in 1540, although only a few knew about it, but a copy was kept in the Jewish community archive in Krakow, and it was recorded in the records of the city of Posen in 1567/8. At the time that the 'deluge' began, i.e. the wars with Sweden (around 1654) which libeled the Jews of the Posen district, Blood Libels concerning Christian children, and the danger of annihilation loomed for the entire Jewish community of that district which had already been diminished even before by the armies of the enemy and the state. Then at that time Rabbi Yaakov, son of Rabbi Naftali of Ganzena, was sent to Rome. He did not succeed in obtaining a letter from the Pope, but he was nevertheless successful in influencing the head of the Dominicans in Rome, Johan di Marinis, the Baptist, who wrote a letter (after about ten years in 1664) to the Priest, Alan Chodrovski, who was the head of this order in Poland. In this letter he demanded that the Dominicans in Poland protect the Jews against these Blood Libels in the church sermons.

A few years later we find the head of other orders writing and warning the heads of states about this matter. And thus the head of the Carmelites, Ferdinand Torgolya, on October 4th 1680 wrote to his representative in Krakow, and on the 22nd of that same month the head of the Augustinians in Rome, Dominicus Velove wrote to the head of this order in Warsaw.

How beneficial these letters were is difficult to determine on the sole basis of documents. They probably helped for a short while and later were covered in obscurity. Therefore there were often repeated efforts to acquire new letters from the Pope and the ranking clergy of the church. Thus we know that when Pope Benedict the 14th in 1751 wrote his infamous letter, the Polish Bishops, Shebmek and Kobilsky, on that basis began to cruelly persecute the Jews. Then too a delegation was sent to Rome and succeeded in influencing the Pope to order his delegate in Warsaw to investigate the matter.

Who were the Jews who stayed in Rome at these times and what were the methods the Jews used? The primary sources, both the Jewish and Christians are silent on these questions. From secondary sources we learnt about this Jewish lobby in Rome, that after the Blood Libel trial in Viterbo (in 1705) a document in Italian and Latin defending the Jews was printed in the Pope's printing house by Rabbi Korkus with legal annotations by the lawyer Alberti. The lobbying Jews tried very hard to obtain these printed documents and to reprint them for the Polish Jews, but it appears that all their work was in vain and they could not obtain even a single copy of these documents. Only later a lone individual, Chayim of Lublin, (descendent of the Alseich family) was successful in getting a copy of these documents. Chayim of Lublin's uncle or cousin was one of the martyrs of Zolmir (Cf. Wolf, 1712) and therefore he took upon himself to obtain the document that vindicated the Jews of the Blood Libel. As he tells us himself, he left his store in Lublin, went to Rome and there he was successful in obtaining the aforementioned documents (for which he paid a very high price) and also the right to translate them and reprint them and indeed, he published them later, in the printing house of Fuerth in Yiddish under the name "Israel's Salvation," taken from the title of Menashe Ben Israel's book.

Whether the Jews of Poland knew about these documents when they sent the above mentioned Rabbi Elyakim to Rome is hard to know, (Rabbi Emden mentions them in the book "Shimush" in the section "Resen Maseh") because the publication date is missing from the title page. Even if the Jews had known about the documents, they did not bring the expected results about which Chaim from Lublin wrote in his introduction to these documents. Rabbi Elyakim, son of Rabbi Asher Zelig from Yampol, had to start the job from the beginning and look for ways and means in which to approach the influential cardinals and bring their attention to the problem of the Jews. For this much money was needed.

The Council of the Four Lands had assigned for him only a small sum, and probably told him to try to get money in Italy. Indeed it was for a good reason that Rabbi Elyakim was called "the representative of the all merciful G-d messenger and of the Four States." A written decision concerning this matter was not found in the archives of the council and apparently never existed, a predicament that caused poor Rabbi Elyakim a lot of trouble and grief.

We do not know the route that Rabbi Elyakim took. We can assume that he made his way through Vienna and Venice and soon enough we find him in Mantua where he gets acquainted with a Jew named Notta and begins to receive money for his goal. It is not known if this Noson or Notta gave Rabbi Elyakim the money as a personal loan to him or if Notta believed that the Four Lands Council would reimburse him, but after a few years Rabbi Elyakim's debt to Notta grew to the amount of 3046 dukats. Notta's patience did not last any longer and with Rabbi Elyakim he turned to the council demanding the reimbursement of his considerable sum of money.

In the meantime Rabbi Elyakim drew on this source, and thanks to this money and with the help of the Rabbis and the Elders of the congregations in Italy (especially in Rome) Rabbi Elyakim was successful in appearing before the papal council.

In Rome, he received much help from the chief rabbi, Rabbi Shabbetai Fiani, who took time away from his many tasks for the sake of his brethren in Poland. From Rome, Rabbi Elyakim prepared a written appeal directed to the Rabbis and communities throughout Italy in which he described his situation and the condition of his oppressed brethren in Poland.

In our hands are found two copies of this manifesto, to Alexandria of Italy and to Kassali. In them we read: "To you distinguished people, I call loudly ... You have known all the grief and troubles that found us since our exile among the Christians, who said that we, G-d forbid, are in need of blood ... and with G-d's mercy for His people, He enlightened the eyes of the Christians - who realized that they had been told a lie about us - but in our area, in Poland this false accusation remains and every once in a while it surfaces again when someone is found dead, and this causes pogroms afflicted on Jewish homes and the spilling of innocent Jewish blood is on the rise..."

One of the Rabbis, Rabbi Elyahu, son of Rabbi Rafael Shlomo from Alexandria, answered Rabbi Elyakim at length and informed him that he knew Cardinal Kovalkini's relatives who used to live in Tortone, and through them he would try to get a letter of recommendation for Rabbi Elyakim and his concerns.

Thanks to his efforts, he succeeded in gaining the attention of Pope Benedict the 14th (who had already, once before, ordered an investigation against Bishop Kobilsky, as a result of the Jews' complaints.) He turned over the Yampol matter into the hands of Cardinal Lorenzo Ganganelli (who later became Pope) in order for him to investigate fully the matter and report before the above mentioned committee. Cardinal Ganganelli hurried to investigate the Jews' complaints at their request, and not only those of the Jews of Yampol but also those of the Jews of Zhitomir and others (from the 1753 trial) that had been put in the archive years before, and already on the 21st of March 1758 he reported and stated his opinion about the whole matter in front of the council. The council accepted Cardinal Ganganelli's findings and sent a letter to the Pope's representative in Warsaw, Mr. Visconti, asking him to investigate the Bishop Soltic of Kiev, Bishop Volovitch of Brisk and Lutzk and also the Jews, residents of the places in which the trials took place.

Thus resurfaced the subject of Zhitomir, and the two Bishops already mentioned were greatly embarrassed as a result of the new trial in Yampol. This time Rome became involved in the matter wishing to investigate the matter itself, especially concerning Soltic, since the rumors that reached Rome about him were very bad.

In this way there came to an end the painful matter of the Blood Libel in Yampol, which had caused a big storm all over the world in all places where oppressed Jews live.

TELL ME
(A call to the Keeper of the cemetery in Yampol)
by Ezriel Goren
(Of Blessed Memory)

[40]

- A -

I remember you, you good, old man
On every Shabbat eve, afternoon,
When mother, bless her memory, took the white loaves
Out of the glowing oven - you appeared
Heavily laden with a sack full of white fragrant Challot.
We, the youngsters kept ourselves distanced from you
And from afar watched your movements as you walked,
Because you diligently watched over the cemetery
Lest it be desecrated. You kept an eye on the gate

That it might not be breached by the shepherds - the wicked.
The heartless with no feelings.
May the dead rest where they lay
Let the fresh grass bloom
And cover with a green carpet
The field of graves of those
Who had departed.
You were treated kindly by Chevra Kadisha
Who, in addition to your place of rest, gave you the right
To knock on the doors of the living
On every eve of Sabbath, and to levy from each household
A warm white Challah, anointed with egg yolk.
Not even a single housewife
Would add, out of the goodness of her heart,
A cube of sugar or a warm doughnut
By way of thanks or loving kindness.
Did you not appear as a messenger, an envoy
And brought silent greetings
From the relatives whose years had ended....
Up there, their memory kept in the hearts of the living.
I still remember, old man, how your bleary eyes
Weeping, your grey face,
Your slovenly walk witnessing and responding:
"Joy has departed our abode."

- B -

And at the end of Sabbath, with darkness ... a funeral -
Through the window we peered, afraid
Weak lights of candle lamps
Lit slightly the darkness of the night,
As a group of bearded Jews
Trudge in the mud.
These are Chevra Kadisha
As they walk and approach the crossing,
A bridge wholly made of willow branches
And black, heavy earth
Which retains a drowning bridge
Between the two "Goryn" river banks.
At the head of the bearers of the bed marches the hatter....
Who only yesterday at Simchat Torah
Appeared in the street with his hat inverted on his head,
And the lining reddened his silvering hair......
Jolly and joking, declaiming aloud:
"Holy flock" - and we, the urchins
Retort after him: "Meh" in deafening sounds.

He pulls out of his pocket a fistful of nuts
Throws them afar, far away,
And the group of mockers swoops
Onto the loot.
The stock has ended, and the group is demanding,
No despair!..... He knocks on the door of the house of the wealthy
Whose wife comes out towards him, a tinge of a smile on her lips, and
Gives him with an open hand a whole dish full of nuts.... and sweets
And the procession continues ....
On the left, holding the pole of the bed
The Treasurer of Chevra Kadisha, Reb Shalom Mantshiles.
A merchant in flax, linen and wool, endowed with sons and daughters,
The eldest among them Hanna Gittl the swarthy beauty, she has
married
Not long ago.
Her heart chosen, an albino young man,
An ardent Zionist who calls meetings together
Recites portions out of "The Jewish State"
And reads out the Resolutions of the First Congress.
And the wise of the township devour every word,
A warm feeling, and a mist of comfort
Hovers and warms the heart of the youngsters
Hearts pound at the thought of the vision.
Even Reb Yossel - the grandson of the Dayan
Sings with emotion in the ears of his young betrothed
"At the cross-roads there lies
A rose with dull red eyes"
Tears flow from their eyes ....
For the Grandfather, the Dayan Reb Doodi, may he rest in peace
Has only just returned from the Land of Israel,
In his pocket the deeds for a house in S'fad.
The third is Yossele, the tinker
The self same Yossele who woke all the Yampol inhabitants
From the sleep of Saturday afternoon
Because of the Samovar, which bubbled and steamed
In the house of Anshel, the apothecary.....
The fourth at the front, Reb Yisroeli Feivishes,
One of the elder learned students,
A favoured teacher of Bible and Gemarra
An enthusiastic Chassid, congregation's delegate and reader of Torah,
Courageous, collector of donations to charity and the one who looks
After the concerns of the town.
In the meantime the grave digger, Reb Isaac the Saddler
Together with the Keeper of the cemetery
Are digging and preparing the ground
For the dear departed.....

- C -

Do you remember, old man, the Keeper,
The gloomy days of autumn?
When the sun glides and hurries
To set in the west far away, far away...
Beyond the chalk hills
And you, poor man shivering, observe from afar
The congregation of Jewish visitors
Men and women in the house of the living!
And here some woman, bitter of heart, kneeling
By the cold stone - the memorial.
She cries and is begging from those
Who rest in their graves,
To arise and to spread their prayers
Before the Creator of the world,
May He look and see from the heavens
Their sorrows and distress.
And you, the dumb one, the bewildered,
How could you know when will arrive
The month of Elul?
It was always engraved in your memory
That the month of visiting and memorials
To the souls of the dead
Coincides with the blowing of the winds of the fall,
With the shedding of leaves
Ushering in the winter and the freeze,
And the dreaming old cemetery,
The one that is across the bay,
With the solitary tent that was raised
Over the graves of the righteous:
Reb Michal of Zloczow may he rest in peace
And his son Reb Yossele, the holy.

- D -

This cemetery is surrounded by a live fence
And is barred with a lock.
Only in the month of Elul
Its gates are opened,
Gates of mercy,
And the righteous - and ordinary Jews,
From near and afar,
Come to prostrate
On the graves of the pious
To ask on their account
For mercy and life.........

Sometimes you pass and cross
The width of the bay, when you swim -
What a depth, and a softness and coolness
In the clear waters of the river Goryn.
You spread your arms
One.... two... and already you hold onto
The live fence of the old cemetery,
You climb and you pass.....
Bewitched from the sight before your eyes
You stand open-mouthed, and you look
At the green carpet
The endless, spread over everything, over all ....
Only a bit here, a snippet there,
Peeps out a stone, a grey monument
Polished by storms and heavy rains,
As if shy behind the grass bridal veil
And here, cornered, between fading tomb stones
Suddenly arises a soft flexible birch,
With its many reversing, glittering colours
With its appearance alternating, sometimes white, and then green.
A little further away arises a young oak,
Sending its weave of roots and branches
In secret and underground,
Into the graves of the sleepers in the soil....
- **E** -
Hear, my old man, faithful and dear
In the cemetery of the Jews !!!!
Lend an ear and hark well
From always until today
You tied your existence, your fate
With the dwellers of the soil
In the long years of your service
You learned that there is contact and co-operation of visits
Between the living and the dead.
The living arrange visits en masse
In the Fall - the month of Elul
And the sleepers in the soil return the visits
Up high, not in large groups, and not at a regular season,
But singly, and in a dream....
Tell me if you can remember
When did the visits cease?
And since when do the headstones lie
Silent deserted and orphaned
These dwellers of the soil?
Only a deep sigh of sorrow,
A sort of wailing of autumn winds,

Breaks out from the depths of their graves
And in answer a dull echo replies
From the depths of the ruined house openings
From a house about to collapse, from a deserted yard,
From a leaking wall, a gaping, orphaned entrance.
And when, tell me, did the accord disappear
The last of the dying
Of an infant and child
Of the old and the infirm?
I, the enlightened, who suckled the culture of Europe,
Ceased to understand what was going on,
The ropes of the wicked entrapped me
I am lost in my despair and my poverty.
- **F** -
Tell me, oh Keeper, after all, most of your days
You spent among the dead, the dwellers of the earth,
And their whispers, from the silence of their grave,
Were cast into your ears as the utterance of lips.
Do you still hear in the middle of the night
A grumble rising from the outskirts of the Yampol ruins,
Why, for what reason, alas!
Did they not bring us to the graves of our fathers?
- **G** -
How does the destroyed town look?
I remember it, the poor robbed place,
An island, an ellipse between Goryn the river
Its source the tributary on the steep slope.
It stands opposite my minds eye,
As always it did before,
Peaceful quiet and beautiful
Divided in squares, three, four
Sectors - suburbs sprawled and compressed
Between the water streams which cut across,
And form a beautiful bay,
Deep and light, which washes
The feet of the old cemetery.
May it be remembered for good, the group of river meadows
There on the plain at the foot of the fort,
Which profits from the floods of Spring
Of the Goryn as it rises,
Which resembles from afar a group of ten Jews
Who pray, tightly packed,
The afternoon prayer in public.
From these river meadows
They tore out filled branches,

For the Lulav palm branch
And festive decor for the synagogue
And for flagellation at Hosha'na Raba.
- **H** -
And the self same vandals,
The children of hell,
The seed of abomination,
A dastardly race
Desecrators of holy,
Purveyors of poison,
Sowers of death,
Hissed by the wildness of the Ukraine,
To be provided with false witness,
To imbibe our blood, the blood of the pure
And to share out the booty,
Your sword was not sharpened
It was not pulled from its sheath,
To hand it to the murderer,
To destroy souls so fast,
You encompassed us with deception and lies,
With a belt of destruction death and despair,
You sowed around us
Fears and dread of death,
Before you murdered us,
Annihilated,
You widened and deepened your crimes,
Crimes of hell,
You played with us a game of blood,
Insolent and criminal.
You slowed down our death throes,
To increase the suffering and pain
Of our sick, aching souls,
Suffering from trouble, distress, the depth of holocaust.
- **I** -
Have you seen, dear Keeper what they have perpetrated,
The wicked, the unclean?
Have you seen the convulsion of bodies
The encrusted blood of the holy, the slain?
Who were burnt alive, killed and destroyed
Though no evil was done by them?
Tell me please, faithful guard!

TSADDIKIM (RIGHTEOUS MEN) AND HIDDEN TSADDIKIM IN YAMPOL
by Rabbi Aharon HaLevy Pichnik

[49]

The town Yampol is well know through its great and famous tsaddikim who achieved a reputation as leaders of the Chassidic movement, each in his generation. This author, who was born in the nearby town of Ostra, and whose grandfather, the tsaddik Rabbi Yaakov-Yosef, Zecher Tsaddik Livracha (may his righteous memory be blessed) found his final resting place in the town of Yampol, heard in his childhood many stories about both the revealed and the hidden tzaddikim of Yampol, and particularly about Rabbi Yechiel Michal, may his memory be blessed, and his son Rabbi Yosef of Yampol who dwelled there for many years.

The Tzaddik Rabbi Yechiel Michal of Zloczow (Of Blessed Memory)

Rabbi Yechiel Michal was born in 5491 (1731) to his father the tzaddik Rabbi Yitzchak of Drohobycz who had lofty lineage, a descendant of Rashi and on through Rabbi Yochanan Hasandlar up to King David, may he rest in peace. Rabbi Yitzchak lived in the days of the Ba'al Shem Tov. At first he opposed the latter's conduct and went to visit and test him. He saw his holy integrity and became a close follower of the Ba'al Shem Tov and brought his young son Rabbi Yechiel Michal to him and he bonded with him in deep love.

After his marriage, Rabbi Michal became a preacher (maggid) in the small town Brusilov, and made a living from the one cow that he had. When his family grew and this was not sufficient for his livelihood, his teacher, the Ba'al Shem Tov, suggested to him that he accept a rabbinical position in a certain city, but because of his extreme modesty, he did not accept the offer. The Ba'al Shem Tov insisted and told him that he would lose his portion in the world [to come] if he continued to refuse, but Rabbi Yechiel Michal replied, "I would be more comfortable losing my portion in the world [to come] rather than wearing a crown which doesn't fit me."

After the Ba'al Shem Tov passed away, Rabbi Yechiel Michal attached himself to the great Maggid Rabbi Dov-Ber of Mezeritch, the disciple and spiritual heir of the Ba'al Shem Tov. By that time he had already been living in Zloczow and very soon after moved to Yampol and became very well known.

The Greatest Tsaddik of the Generation

Rabbi Avraham Yehoshua Heshel of Apt (Opatow) used to say: "Every generation has one righteous person to whom the key of the Torah is given. In our time, I didn't know who was that righteous man of this generation until I came to Rabbi Yechiel Michal, the preacher of Zloczow. As soon as he opened his mouth and expounded upon words of the Torah, all the doubts I had were gone. Then I knew that the key of the Torah was in his hands and he, indeed, is the most righteous of the generation."

Chassidim tell that Rabbi Abraham Yehoshua Heshel of Apt used to come every once in a while to Yampol to his friend Rabbi Yechiel Michal who, as is well known, was very poor and did not want to derive pleasure from this world. Rabbi Yechiel Michal was also a Torah scholar, spending all his days at home studying the Torah and in religious devotion, whereas Rabbi Abraham Yehoshua Heshel would wander from place to place. Once when Rabbi Abraham Yehoshua Heshel came to see his friend Rabbi Yechiel Michal and saw the poverty in which he lived his life, he asked him why he was not willing to visit his followers from time to time, and thus would have a comfortable income. "And how is it with you?" asked Rabbi Yechiel Michal. "Not only do I have enough for my sustenance, I even have silver and gold dishes" answered Rabbi Abraham Yehoshua Heshel from Apt. "Well then" answered Rabbi Yechiel Michal, "I would rather sit at my home while the gold and silver is elsewhere than wander from place to place while the gold and silver in my home."

Although Rabbi Yechiel Michal had many disciples from near and far, and he spread chassidism among the masses of the Jews, he aroused the anger of the Mitnagdim (opposers of chassidism) who were strong in Zloczow and he was forced to move from Zloczow, becoming a maggid in Yampol which was then a town full of Torah and piety and whose rabbi was then the famous scholar and author of the Noda BiYehuda, Rabbi Yechezkel Landau.

The Mitnagdim (opposers) reached him there too, and wrote hateful letters about him to the Rabbi of Yampol, the Noda BiYehuda, saying that he, Rabbi Yechiel Michal, did not pray on time and made light of many mitzvot. But Rabbi Yechiel Michal's colleague, the Gaon, Rabbi Pinchas Horowitz, author of the Talmudic commentary "Hafla'ah," wrote a personal letter to the town's Rabbi in which he defended Rabbi Yechiel Michal and said that "all his deeds are for G-d's sake". As a result, Rabbi Yechezkel Landau ordered that he was not to be bothered and was to be allowed to worship G-d as he saw fit. Only then did the dispute quieten down.

As it is known, Rabbi Yechezkel Landau left the town of Yampol in 5515 (1755) and went to Prague to officiate in that honorable position.

Thus we can conclude that Rabbi Yechiel Michal resided in Yampol for more than 30 years till he died there in 5546 (1785).

The Five Books of the Torah

Rabbi Yechiel Michal had five sons and one daughter. The sons who were famous Tzaddikim and founded their own Chassidic dynasties were: Rabbi Yosef, who inherited his father's place in Yampol, Rabbi Moshe of Zvehil, Rabbi Yitzchak of Radzivill, Rabbi Ze'ev of Zbariz, and Rabbi Mordecai of Kremenetz. Rabbi Yechiel Michal's sons were known in the Chassidic literature by the name 'The five books of the Torah' since each corresponded to one of the books of the Torah. His son, Rabbi Ze'ev from Zbarov, was called "Vayikra" (Leviticus) because he was known as a 'perfect offering' and many stories are told about his pure character. The family name of Rabbi Mordecai of Kremenetz was "Mishnah" after the book of Deuteronomy (called Mishnah Torah).

The name of Rabbi Yechiel Michal's only daughter was Yentl and the Tzaddikim of that era said that she was inspired with "Ruach Hakodesh" (the spirit of G-d). Chassidim would recall that a few times during her work in the kitchen or at home she stopped working and jumped three times saying "Kadosh, Kadosh, Kadosh!" When asked why she did this she said that she had heard angels arranging the "kedusha" in front of G-d and together with them she said "Kadosh."

Concerning her match, it was told that when she was eleven years old, her mother, the Rebbetsin, went to her husband Rabbi Yechiel Michal and told him that their only daughter had come of marriageable age and it was necessary to pray for the proper match for her. Her husband answered that G-d, blessed be He, would undoubtedly bring to their home the appropriate match.

Among Rabbi Yechiel Michal's pupils was Rabbi David, the Maggid of Stepan, a man who was one of the brilliant pupils of the great maggid Rabbi Dov Ber from Mezeritch. After his mentor passed away, Rabbi David turned to Yampol to be Rabbi Yechiel Michal's disciple. Rabbi David used to walk from Stepan, in Volhyn, to his Rabbi. One day as he approached Yampol, a messenger from Rabbi Yechiel Michal came to him and told that his Rabbi was waiting for him and that he should go straight to him.

When he reached town, Rabbi David did not go to his usual hostel, but rather turned immediately to his Rabbi's house to know why the latter summoned him with such urgency. Rabbi Yechiel Michal explained to him explicitly that he saw him as his only daughter's match and he asked him to be his son-in-law. Upon hearing these words Rabbi David was astonished since he was already forty years old and his first wife who had died, had left him with four young children, and he knew that his Rabbi's daughter was still very young. However he immediately recovered and said that if his Rabbi chose him to be a husband to his daughter, he would certainly agree.

Then, Rabbi Yechiel Michal called his wife to his room and pointing at Rabbi David, he said "This is our daughter's mate." The Rebbetzen almost fainted out of fear that such an old man, who had young children, was to be their young daughter's husband. But Rabbi Yechiel Michal spoke to her softly saying "You know what? We will call the girl and ask her. She will know if he is the right partner for her or not." To this the Rebbetzen agreed. They called their daughter who looked at the man and immediately said "Yes."

From the marriage of Yentl, Rabbi Yechiel Michal's only daughter, to Rabbi David, the preacher from Stepan, were born a few sons and daughters among them: Rabbi Israel-Dov, the "young maggid" of Stepan, and Rabbi Yechiel Michal Pichnik (this author's grandfather), who founded the Chassidic dynasty of the Volhynian town of Brezna (Berezno.)

The Sayings, Interdictions and Teachings of Rabbi Yechiel Michal

Of the famous sayings of Rabbi Yechiel Michal, I quote here a few:

"All the Mitzvot are given in the Torah as commandments except for Humility that is mentioned as praise to Moshe Rabeynu, because real humility is when a person really feels that he is small and lowly and he does something just because it is a mitzvah.

"Whoever G-d loves He will reprimand" (Proverbs 3, 12) can also be read "Whoever who loves G-d will reprimand Him" for not redeeming His children (the Jews) from being in exile for such a long time.

With regard to his reason for being late with his prayers Rabbi Yechiel Michal used to say: "The tribe of Dan walked last because they were the rear guard of all the camps and they picked up all the things that the ones walking in front of them had lost and brought them back to their owners. So also I am praying last and I am gathering all the lost and abandoned prayers and am raising them back to the source."

"Tzaddikim do not have any rest either in this world or in the world to come" [Psikta Zutrasi], this is because only something which requires exertion is relevant to fatigue and rest, but the righteous who worship G-d do not get tired and therefore need no rest.

"I stand between G-d and you" [Deut. 5, 5], whoever has pride and thus is in the category of "I", this stands between G-d and himself, creating a barrier that stands between him and his Father in heaven.

"I never needed anything which I did not yet have," said Rabbi Yechiel Michal, "because as long as I did not have it, I knew that apparently I did not need it."

There are two kinds of worship. One with Torah [study], prayer and the fear of G-d, and one with [worship through] material matters. But first it is necessary to start with Torah and with worshipping G-d spiritually, and through this to suppress the evil inclination, then one is permitted to start the worship of G-d even through the mundane.

"Thou shalt be Holy because I am Holy" [Lev. 19,2.] On this our sages commented [Medrash rabbah] "'Because I am Holy', My holiness is above your holiness" and Rabbi Yechiel Michal said these enigmatic words, 'who doesn't know that G-d's holiness is higher?' But the meaning is "My Holiness above - the holiness of G-d above - is from your holiness, - according to how you sanctify Me below - as it is written "Give strength to G-d!" [Psalms 68, 35].

A few examples of his religious counsels:
    a) Be careful not to embarrass even a person known to be wicked.
    b) Be careful to go to sleep wearing tsitsit and not too much clothing.
    c) Be careful of studying the Agada (homiletic passages in Rabbinic literature) or the Zohar (the book of Kabbalah) prior to going to sleep.
    d) Be careful to avoid gossip, slander, mockery, lies and useless talk.
    e) Stay as far away as possible from anger and melancholy.
    f) Pray from the Siddur [and not by heart], facing the wall and with full Kavanah (devotion).
    g) Be careful to answer "Amen. Yehei shmei rabah ... [Let His great name be blessed (During the Kaddish)]" with all your might and kavanah.
    h) Be careful not to talk in the synagogue, especially when the congregation is praying.
    i) Be careful to avoid desecrating the Sabbath even through speech.
The Chassidim also used to say that Rabbi Yechiel Michal was very careful about three things:
He never warmed up near the stove because this causes a person to be lazy.
He never scratched or rubbed his body because this brings about the degeneration of the body.
He never bent his head down to eat, but rather raised the food to his mouth.

He said that whoever can be careful about these things, this is a clear sign that he is a descendent of King David's royal family.

Rabbi Yechiel Michal's Passing Away

The Chassidim tell that he passed away on the Sabbath day, the 25th of Elul, 5546 (1785). That day he came to the synagogue to pray. They called him up to the Torah and it was the Sabbath of the combined Nitzavim - Vayelech portions of the Torah. They honored him with the sixth Aliyah and they read before him: "Behold the days approach that thou must die..." [Deut. 31, 14 (which is in the sixth Aliya of that Torah reading)] and he was 55 years old, equal to the numerical value of the word "Hen [Behold]".

He knew then that his end was near and he began to advise his family of his will. On that same day during the third meal (se'uda shlishit) he walked back and forth and said loudly: "It was in this [revelation of Divine] will that Moses departed from the world [Zohar Yisro 88b]" and he (Rabbi Yechiel Michal) left this world.

The Tzaddikim of his time told that at the time of his death the celestial court called out and declared that the greatest Tzaddik of the generation had passed away and that all the Tzaddikim would go to meet him, and the Ba'al Shem Tov and all his disciples came out to welcome him with love and affection. May the memory of the Tzaddik be a blessing. He is buried in the city of Yampol.

The Tzaddik RABBI YOSEF FROM YAMPOL
(Of Blessed Memory)

Rabbi Yechiel Michal's son, Rabbi Yosef, or as they fondly called him, Rabbi Yossel Yampoller, filled his father's position in Yampol. He never stopped studying the Torah, and they said about him that not only was he an expert in the "Shas" (the entire Talmud) and "Poskim" (halachic codes) but also in The Guide for the Perplexed (by Maimonides) as well as in other philosophical works.

Rabbi Yosef was a friendly man who liked every Jew as himself. I heard about many Chassidic Rabbis who used to go in the month of Elul to Yampol in order to visit Rabbi Yossel's grave. Rabbi Yossef also had a pleasant voice and his prayers were fiery.

In the famous Kether Shem Tov ("Crown of a Good Name", an anthology of the teachings of the Ba'al Shem Tov) the miraculous story is told of how on the day of the passing of the pious Rabbi Yechiel Michal, Rabbi Yossef, his son, suddenly fell ill because an accusation had been aroused against him in heaven claiming that his prayers were not entirely motivated for the sake of G-d. Then he heard in his dream an announcer saying "Go all you righteous souls to welcome the holy Rabbi, Rabbi Yechiel Michal from Zloczow." Rabbi Yossef saw how all the righteous headed by Rabbi Yisroel the Ba'al Shem Tov met with his father and he heard his father saying to the Ba'al Shem Tov: "My son, Yossef, is standing now before the court in heaven." The Ba'al Shem Tov went and stood before the celestial court and said: "What do you have against my dear Yossef?"

The prosecutor says that his praying is not pure? I tell you, let him pray in front of you and you'll see his prayer."

Later the Ba'al Shem Tov turned to Rabbi Yossef and said "Yossef, my son, pray before the Creator and He will help you." Rabbi Yossef started to pray with tremendous enthusiasm, and as a result he started to sweat and he woke up, recovered and lived. All this is in the book Kether Shem Tov quoting "Nethiv Mitzvotecha," - "And still in our days one could see on the lectern in the synagogue in Yampol an antique tablecloth full of Rabbi Yossef's tears, the ones he shed during his enthusiastic praying, full of spirit and longing." The Gabaim (officers of the synagogue) were afraid to remove the tablecloth that absorbed the sighs and tears of this pious man to exchange it for another one.

And in the book "The Noda BiYehuda and his teachings" (the new revised edition published by Mosad HaRav Kook, Jerusalem 1962) written by Rabbi A.L.Gellman, a native of Yampol, the following is told about Rabbi Yossef of Yampol (chapter I, page 2): "The author of the Noda Biyehuda mentions him in his book "Tslach" [an acronym for "Tsiun Lenefesh Chaya"] (tractate Betza Chapter I page 5b) "for more than forty years ago the great sharpwitted rabbi, Rabbi Yossef of the holy community of Yampol posed the following question ...."

Besides his greatness in the Torah and Chassidism, he was also a religious philosopher, an expert in "The Guide to the Perplexed" and other religious philosophical works. Rabbi Yitzchak Ber Levinson (RIBA'L), author of Beth Yehuda, Teuda BeYisroel, Zerubavel, Efes Damim, etc., lived in Yampol for three years during Rabbi Yossef's lifetime and afterwards moved to Kremenetz. As is well known, Rabbi Yitzchak Ber Levinson was one of the strong opposers of Chassidism. Only once did he visit Rabbi Yossef, when he and a friend of his did not understand one of the articles in Maimonides' Guide for the Perplexed. When they came to him and set forth their difficulty, he provided a satisfactory solution. RIBA'L then said that he regretted that he had not visited Rabbi Yossef before.

Rabbi Yossef served as the Chassidic Leader in the town of Yampol for over twenty five years. He died there with a good reputation in

1812, and was buried near his father's grave, in the old cemetery in the town of Yampol.

Rabbi Yaakov-Yosef of Ostra
(Of Blessed Memory)

Among the righteous who came to Yampol for the yearly memorial ceremony to pray on Rabbi Yossef's grave was the well known rabbi, Rabbi Yaakov-Yosef of Ostra, the grandson of Rabbi Yi'vi [i.e. Rabbi Yaakov-Yossef I of Ostra, author of the book of chassidic teachings, called Rabbi Yi'vi" after his initials], a disciple of the Ba'al Shem Tov and the Maggid of Mezeritch, who passed away in Yampol [i.e. Rabbi Yaakov-Yossef II] on the eve of the holy Sabbath, the 23rd of of Tammuz, 5609 [1849].

According to the stories of the Chassidim, Rabbi Yaakov-Yosef often expressed his wish to be buried near the graves of the righteous Rabbi Yechiel Michal and his son Rabbi Yossef, in Yampol. In 5509 [1849], he went to spend the Sabbath in the town of Yampol and there, suddenly he died, on Friday the 23rd of Tammuz, close to noon time. The journey from Yampol to Ostra takes about six hours of travelling. Messengers were sent to bring his kittel (white surplice worn on High Holidays and in which a man is buried) from Ostra and a miracle happened to them. They experienced a miraculous shortening of the journey and were able to go and return with his kittel, and there was still time to arrange for the funeral and return from the cemetery before the Sabbath arrived.

The Chassidim of Ostra, of whom there were many in Yampol and who had their own Beit Medrash [synagogue and study hall] there, were known to be sharpwitted and learned people who also liked to drink and spend time in Chassidic gatherings. It was said that they had in them a Volhynian version of "Kotzk Chassidism." This Rabbi Yaakov-Yosef, who was buried honorably in Yampol, created the popular Chassidic movement of Ostra and his fame and good name spread throughout the region.

Rabbi Yaakov-Yosef was always preaching in praise of the Jewish people and their redemption from the hands of foreign people. He would explain the words of our sages, "There is no difference between this world and the days of the Messiah except the oppression of Israel by kingdoms" (Talmud Berachot 34), that before the arrival of the Messiah will come the 'days of the Messiah' and in these days, Israel will get back their kingdom and they will not be oppressed by foreign kingdoms and only after living an independent life will they be prepared to welcome the Messiah."

Rabbi Yaakov-Yossef explained this in a parable, which was nice and to the point: "There was a poor porter who worked very hard all winter in order to prepare himself for the many expenses of Passover. He saved of his daily bread and even rented himself out as a night watch man. He worked day and night non-stop. Even on the eve of the holiday he was occupied and busy, bringing in all that was needed for the holiday till close to the evening when he still managed to run to the mikvah and afterwards get to the synagogue to pray. When he returned home, he was happy to see that everything was ready and at hand for him for the Seder and he went and sat on the reclining couch and made the blessing over the wine. As soon as he drank the glass of wine, the fatigue of all his winter work descended on him and he fell asleep and slumbered. His wife tried to wake him up pleading, 'You worked and labored so hard all the time in order to reach these happy moments when the whole family is reclining around the Seder table. How can you let all your labor be in vain?' However he was not able to hear her because of his great weariness and their joy was interrupted. It is the same way with our depressed and oppressed people," said Rabbi Yaakov-Yossef. "We are very tired of the exile and the oppression and if the Messiah will come all of a sudden, we will not be able to welcome him and accept all the goodness. We will fall into a deep sleep and all will be in vain."

"Therefore, it is necessary to get rid of all the oppression of the foreign kingdoms and to emigrate to Zion joyfully, to live a full life with each person under his own vine and fig-tree, and then we will be able to welcome the Messiah the proper way."

Rabbi Yaakov-Yossef would speak harshly against the rule of the Czar in Russia, for he passed evil decrees upon Israel. He used to say that in heaven they had already thrown the ruler of Russia off his throne and he had no hope of returning to rule. However just as a big wheel that is being pushed keeps on rolling for a while, so the regime of the wicked Czar will continue a little longer as a result of the push that it received when it was thrown down.

Now we see that his prediction came true, but then when his words reached the authorities, an order was issued to arrest Rabbi Yaakov-Yossef and two other famous Tsaddikim, Rabbi Israel of Rizhin and Rabbi Abraham of Trisk, who had also spoken harshly against the wicked ruling authorities. Rabbi Yaakov-Yossef sat in prison for more than half a year until his Chassidic followers and his admirers succeeded in setting him free.

In my childhood, at the home of my maternal grandfather Tzaddik Rabbi Alteroni, the grandson of Rabbi Yaakov-Yossef, in Ostra, I heard from an elderly Chassid who had known Rabbi Yaakov Yossef and was his follower, that once, on Rosh Hashana before the blowing of the

Shofar Rabbi Yaakov-Yossef remained in his room for a longer time than usual. Afterwards he came into the synagogue, went up to the bima and began with these words: "Gentlemen! I'll tell you a story. In my house there was a custom to buy every day a pennyworth of sweets for the children, and because there were nine children and only enough sweets for eight, they used to say to the oldest boy Getzel (Rabbi Yaakov-Yossef's eldest son, Rabbi Elyakim Getzel, who inherited his place) who was a very wise boy, "You are wise enough to know that your father cannot spend any more money for sweets, therefore you should forgo your share." Since they repeated this chorus every day, this oldest son (Rabbi Elyakim Getzel) came once into my room, burst out crying and said to me 'What sin did I commit that I am wise? It is worthwhile to be stupid once, and get my share!' Then Rabbi Yaakov-Yossef broke into tears, repeated these last words his son said and began Lamenatzeach [psalm 47, which is recited before blowing the Shofar] ..."

Rabbi Yaakov-Yossef's last name was Sfarad and it was said that there is a family tradition that they were descendants of the exiled Jews of Spain, and thirteen generations after them, up to Rabbi Yaakov-Yossef, were possessed of divine inspiration.

Rabbi Leib Naphcha

A wonderful man, in Yampol, was Rabbi Leib Koval (Naphcha) about whom it was said that he was one of the thirty-six hidden Tzaddikim in the world. He occupied himself all his life, building a carriage to go out and welcome the Messiah, the king. He used to stand all day long in his workshop, preparing this carriage, beautifying it and improving it in order to be ready to go out with it to welcome the Messiah.

One year a rumor spread throughout the Jewish world, attributed to the Tzaddikim of the generation, that according to all the signs, that year was the year the Messiah would come. Rabbi Leib then would wear his festive Sabbath clothes every day and stand at the door of his workshop awaiting the coming of the herald's voice, so that he could take his carriage and go to greet the Messiah.

When the year passed and the Messiah had not come, Rabbi Leib took apart the carriage and closed his workshop. He then joined his forefathers, departing from life in this world. They buried him near the wall of the structure over Rabbi Yaakov Yossef's grave.

A few other righteous rabbis found their last resting place in Yampol. Among them were Rabbi Yechiel Michal of Szhumsk, Rabbi Meir, the grandson of Rabbi Yaakov-Yossef of Ostra, and others from the family of Rabbi Yechiel Michael of Zloczow. The old cemetery in

Yampol, as well as the new cemetery, were full of tombstones of great and holy rabbis. Now though, with Yampol in the hands of the Soviets, and after experiencing the wave of conquest and occupation by the Nazis, may their name be blotted out, and the total destruction and extermination of the Jewish population there, who knows if the markers and the tombstones of the great righteous and learned rabbis of Yampol are still there, the rabbis who shed great light in the Jewish world over many generations. May their memory be blessed.

JEWISH TOWN *
by Yehudit Kalish

[59]
Dear son, you ask: "What is a town?"
"And why, mother, do you speak this word with trembling and fear?
And why do you have these pearls of tears beneath your eyes?
And why, tell me mother, has your face changed?"
"Because the town, the town already belongs to the past -
Only a warm drop of it remains in my heart
And as a wonderful dream it floats up in my memory,
This why I suffer, and tremble with tears my son!"
A weekday in the town, how much holiness it absorbed
And so much more on Shabbat and even more on holidays.
Joy in the family was everyone's joy.
Mourning shall envelop everything, one single mourner.
Here rise and shown as in an exhibition
Many pictures distilled from sadness and joy.
Such that without government and order they stand as testimony
And testify to the purity of Jewish life.
A small alleyway meanders around it easily and gaily
Among slightly decrepit wood houses...and my eyes still see
To where has Grandma Zissel hurried off. And what is there in her basket?
She nods her head to me without making her voice heard...
The edge of our grandma's hair ornament delicately flaps
It looks like she folded in her seventy years and hid them inside...
Now her steps are light, she lowers her eyes
She hurried to the edge of town, with a basket of Shabbat goods.
To poor Elkeleh, consumed with suffering.
And to Rabbi Yosef the Blind (they say he is a hidden saint)
Woven challah bread in a warm hand, and wine for Kiddush
A portion of fish and a little meat, the basket is filled
She slipped away, disappeared in the maze of the alley and path
There only remains the echo of a mitzvah [good deed], light and joy.
*From a long poem in the journal "Bait Yaakov".

Soon the ear will hear the dull echo of footsteps,
Arose a second picture like a witness stand,
Here, a little study hall looks innocently at me,
Full of the innocent breath of babes in study,
And it is full of life and saturated with Torah.
Absorbing pure fear of G-d
Shaking my bones and making my soul tremble.
As I talk about it, my dear son, my head gets heavy;
The cold outside penetrates my bones
But here, inside the miniature Temple are warm, very warm
Teacups of Itzik David, the scholar
And warmer than everything is the flowing tune
The very ancient tune of Gemarra [Talmud], a wonderful eternal song.
Many murmurs of repentance settling on your conscience.
And the tune plays on the chords of the sinful soul,
He creates value there, on every note he will scratch
Yes, I shall remind you of my study hall of weekdays and Shabbat,
You were the heart of the town, we guarded you in a moment
And when your voice went silent, Oy! And in a flame up to heaven
You went up, but you remained the pulse of our life...
A third picture, not clear, they covered it with mist
Morning has not yet dawned, everything is covered in shadows.
And who is there, walking and hurrying with song?
Yes, that is the town beadle, always, always first.
He was the first to break out and rise from the alley.
Knocking on every window of shack and shed
Waking those asleep and this is what he said:
"Arise good Jews, to serve G-d."
And when the sun later rose to shine on the Earth,
It blessed the labor of the spots of the faces of the pure,
In the market it toured from stall to stall,
Because the market too was a tabernacle of faith and simplicity.
It even wanted to give enjoyment to the coachmen
It listened to the common talk of those sitting on the benches.
Even from there it occasionally sent a shining pearl,
Since even the very simple folk of those days were of a different sort...
And many more pictures, more and more,
What good is to describe or tell
If from all of this nothing remains
There remains only the sorrow in my heart: "How she sits alone [The first
words of the Book of Lamentations]."
And now, my son, do you understand what a town is?
And why this words comes on my lips with trembling and fear?
And why I have pearls of tears under my eyes?
And why my face has changed this way?----

Because the town, the town already belongs to the past,
Only a warm drop of it remains in my heart.

THE YAMPOL CHRONICLES
I Believe
by Rabbi Shimon Effrati

[62]

'Habakuk came and pitched them [the Mitzvot] all on one foundation "the righteous shall live by his faith" (Habakuk 2,4) (end of tractate Makkos 24a.)

(I)

To every nation serious plights occur which endanger their existence, and the immutable condition to their continued existence and their overcoming the hardships of the times is that they believe with all their spiritual strength in their role in the world. They must accomplish it, and for that purpose they are prepared to sacrifice their lives, to battle and to emerge victorious. The faith of a nation is its soul. From its trust in the truth of its faith it draws strength and fortitude to beat back all those which threaten its existence. When it loses its faith in its perpetuity its foundation is pulled out from under its survival, and its end is annihilation.

In a similar manner the "Rosh" [Rabbenu Asher] explains the halachic principle of "kol d'alim gvar" [the stronger shall overcome, i.e. when two litigants come before a court with an article being held by both of them and both claim possession, the halacha is that whoever is strong enough to physically wrest the article away from his opponent takes possession of it.] The "Rosh" writes: Don't imagine that our Holy Torah, all of whose ways are pleasant [Proverbs 3,17] would give preference to the power of the fist, and declare it victorious in judgement. The truth is that this law of "kol d'alim gvar" is a special concept which derives from the human and ethical 'spring' which is imprinted upon the noble soul of Man which comes from a Holy source. The implication is that when an evil person rises against you to rob you and steal that which is yours, which you have toiled for with the sweat of your brow, then even if he is apparently stronger than you, you will battle with him with all your soul and muster up all your strength, conscious and unconscious, the revealed and the hidden, that known to you and that unknown even to you, and eventually you will be able to overcome brute strength and emerge victorious. This is true both of individuals and of nations.

But there is faith and there is faith. Some believe outwardly, others believe inwardly. There are those whose faith is superficial. He believes as if he believes, but his faith is only lip service, 'the mitzvah of people who learned by rote' [Isaiah 29, 13.] The prophet says: "the righteous shall live by his faith" [Habakuk 2,4.] This means that his own faith shall be his faith, which springs forth from the depths of his soul. There are nations, great and small, who declared their faith before all, and sang its praise without relent, but they did not withstand the trial when put to the test, and one day rose and threw it out from before them as an unwanted utensil and exchanged it for another and clove to the other.

Not so the portion of Jacob! The Jewish religion is the oldest on earth, and it is also the newest and the youngest. Its freshness and relevance is as the day of its birth. Even more, today it is more relevant than ever, it stands today in the open and points a finger at the place of shame of the sick, loathsome and wounded humanity. It determines both the diagnosis and the prognosis, and points to both the place of shame and the place of recovery. As the Ba'al Shem Tov interpreted the words of Rabbi Yehoshua ben Levi in Avoth ch. VI "Every day a Heavenly voice goes forth from Mount Horeb proclaiming 'Woe to humanity for the disgrace of the Torah.'" The Ba'al Shem Tov explains: the 'Woe' the sickness and the loathsomeness, the destruction and the annihilation, which have come upon humanity, their source is the disgrace of the Torah. They ignored the voice of the Torah, they have disobeyed the seven Mitzvot which were commanded to all the children of Noah. They have not shaken off the coarse dust of idolatry and their other abominations. And here is a clear directive on how to prepare for the coming of evil in the future.

(II)

Indeed, we shall loudly proclaim before all comers - not because we the smallest of nations, the weakest and most dispersed of peoples, have they risen against from all sides to swallow us alive, and our enemies and pursuers have multiplied. Rather because we are the spiritually strongest of nations. Because we are a great and mighty people. Because we have the strength of a true religion. "Sinai, wherefrom hatred [Sina] came down to Israel" [Shabbos 89b.]

The accursed Nazis, and with them all other evil gentiles, did not fall upon us with anger and fury and unparalleled cruel wickedness because we were weaker than them, but because we were better than them. They, the profane wicked, killed our Holy martyrs not because they propagated typhus bacteria and plagues, but because even in their crowdedness they radiated rays of light and seeds of Holiness which those profane ones could not tolerate.

They invaded attics where school children were studying Torah in choked voices. As long as that voice is heard in the world the demon Ashmadai cannot live in peace. They burnt down Jewish homes in the cities because they felt with their beastly instinct that those homes were the nest of a heritage of many generations of longing to pure life, of fear of sin and awe of Heaven, in the very loftiest sense. They commanded children to be placed before hungry dogs before their mothers' eyes because from the glance of a day old child righteousness already shone and blinded the eyes of the wicked.

Their cruel hearts exalted with pleasure at seeing human bodies dragged with iron chains from the gas chambers, because after thousands of years of superficial and counterfeit 'culture' the beast within them saw with its beastly instinct that we were a creature higher than them. For this can they not feel an eternal hatred and can they not avenge themselves upon us with cruel wrath? Thus we have paid with our blood and souls a high price for our advantage and splendor.

I stood before this Mount Moriah which is more sacred than Mount Sinai since on it Jews stretched out their necks went upon the flaming altar to die at "Echod" a martyr's death. I was in several of the cities of death and I saw and heard the song of wrath of the victors and of the vanquished. Sometimes I close my eyes and I see before me the picture that I saw all over Europe on rivers of blood and tears of our unfortunate nation. There stands before me an entire congregation with the rabbi at their head, some garbed in Tallitim under their coats, in front of the bunkers and pits that they dug with their own hands. And here among the groups stands an unfortunate mother. Beside her is her lovely child with golden locks. She stands upright and with a spirit of disdain toward those standing behind them, weapons in hand, standing prepared as depraved priests of idolatry ready to offer sacrifices to their idol Molech. But they are dwarves against these giants of the spirit who know and believe that from between the layers of clouds the sun will again shine, and these murderers will not succeed in reinstating the reign of darkness over the world.

Thus, with their death, they bequeathed us with lives of sanctity and purity. They upon the flames with wondrous devotion, while in their hearts burned their great faith and in their mouths was the song of the hope of complete redemption "although he tarrieth I believe and await him." They were sure that we are standing not only at the end of a long period of bitter exile, but also at the edge of redemption, and if they would not merit seeing it their brothers and sisters would. They accepted upon themselves the verdict in order that through their death the entire nation would be atoned.

(III)

Now the bitter, burning, and very painful question arises. What has the great and exalted Jewish people done to commemorate the names of the holy and pure martyrs who fell on the altar of the nation? Not only have we not erected fitting memorial monuments, but we have abandoned them to the teeth of wild dogs and sick humans. Their bones are spread out across the earth of the profane nations of Europe, where every grain of earth is soaked with the blood and tears of our martyred brethren.

I believe with perfect faith that if we have been privileged, the nations of the world have recognized our right to our homeland, it is only in the merit of that tribe which was sacrificed as a burnt offering, in the merit of these martyrs who believed with perfect faith in the redemption of Israel.

OUR FRIENDLY VILLAGE, YAMPOL
by Yaacov Horzshach
(Of Blessed Memory)
(Parts One and Two)

[65]

To my dear and valued fellow ex-Yampolites! It is for you that I write these lines. The fate that befell hundreds and thousands of the villages of Poland Galitzia, Latvia and the Ukraine is not in the realm of the living.

Our village Yampol was one of those. The cruel enemy, the evil Nazis, did not pass her by. They exterminated and burned all our friends and relatives, our sisters and brothers. Except for a few individuals out of hundreds, who were miraculously saved, not one remains. The animals [Nazis] exterminated them and swept them off the face of the earth. Years will pass and from our village there will not remain, heaven forbid, any remembrance for future generations. Our children, and the children of our children will not know that in the world of the Holy One, blessed be He, it happened that their loved ones and dear ones were exterminated in such a cruel and horrible way.

Because of this, I have taken upon myself, the son of your village who you still remember from there, the task and trouble to go forth and write down lines and remembrances, in order to erect a modest monument to the memories of all those who were destroyed and are gone.

It is hard to answer with any exactitude the question: "How old was our town Yampol?" because no one remembered or wrote down when and by whom the village was founded, who laid the foundations and who were its first settlers, but there is no doubt that the village was several thousand years old. The hundreds of ancient and faded gravestones in the old graveyard in the village bore witness to this fact.

This graveyard was situated on the other side of the western road, close to the southern bank of the river. It is possible that hundreds of years ago the graveyard was a great distance from the river. It is possible that perhaps with the passage of time, the water shifted the banks of the river towards the graveyard.

Even our old folks did not remember when we started using the new graveyard that was around four kilometers from the village on the side of the road to the village of Pinkovich. Despite this, the old folks used to say, at every opportunity and with great enjoyment, that several hundred years ago, our village was renowned in all the area because the famous Gaon, Rabbi Yechezkel Landau, known in the rabbinical world as "Noda BiYehudah" (literally "known in Judea") ran the Rabbinate here for ten years.

[Footnote: the writer, who was born and educated in Yampol, started writing an entire book about the village. To our sorrow, death claimed him first. He died a peaceful death in Buenos Aires, Argentina. Only the first two chapters have come into our possession.]

Some words on this subject were found in the ancient village ledger, that was in the possession of the Gabbai of the Chevra Kadisha. To my regret, I never got to see this ledger, but my Uncle Shalom, of blessed memory, who was known as Shalom Batsheles, was for many years the Gabbai of the Chevra Kadisha, and the village ledger was always in his possession. He used to peer into it from time to time.

I remember that my uncle told me that in that ledger were written several references to the fact that Rabbi Yechezkel Landau was our village leader during his tenure in the village Rabbinate.

It is easy to assume that with his departure from our Rabbinate, the village felt a great loss. It is also hard to believe that because of this all the town's spiritual life, which had been in existence for a long time before his tenure, was cut off. However, it did flower and grow during the years of his Rabbinate.

In the period following the Rabbinate of Rabbi Yechezkel, we can only grope in the darkness, because there are no surviving writings on our village's life, development and growth over the last one hundred and fifty years. Therefore I will not engage in investigations and assumptions in this matter.

THE NOBLE'S COURT

The town of Yampol, and the surrounding countryside, including the rivers, four mills, forests and fields, belonged for generations to a family of Polish nobles and passed by inheritance from father to son, or to other relatives if there were no sons.

The last heir of all this property was the Polish noble Lampitzky, a respected noble who lived all his life with his wife (they had no children) abroad, reputedly in Paris. From time to time he would come to our village and visit his property, to check if everything was going well. Afterwards he would once again disappear for a long while.

While the noble couple lived as foreigners in the 'exile' they took upon themselves, their palace in our village was kept up in every detail. The maids and servants baked and cooked. The grooms and groundsmen cleaned and polished the horses and carriages. The guards and gardeners cultivated and perfected the palace gardens, and everything carried on as if they were awaiting the imminent return of 'their Excellencies.' Everything had to be correct and in its place.

The Nobles' property was overseen for years by a Pole by the name of Yakobovski. He was a rotund fellow, short and pleasant-faced. He used to answer his acquaintances' greetings with a friendly smile, ready to engage in longer conversation. Except for a small tax which the homeowners had to pay to the Noble Lampitsky, which was levied by Yakobovski, the two had no other dealings. The only one who had close relations with the 'Court,' that is with the Nobleman, was the 'Lord' of our village, David Kertman, who was usually called "David Shayas" (Isaiah's David.)

This David Shayas was the Trustee and chief inspector of the Noble's property. Even Yakobovski had to report to him about everything he did. This report, along with his comments and explanations were delivered to the Noble along with the sum of money the couple needed for living expenses abroad.

Another person who had professional dealings with the 'Court' was the rich man of the town, Barish Baruchs. For as long as I can remember, he leased the large village flour mill, and two other small mills in the neighboring villages. The Noble took no part in their operation, because they were arranged by the manager Yakobovski or by David Shayas, and the Noble only knew what his trustees chose to tell him after the fact.

The 'Court' included a beautiful palace, tall and wide, and all of one story, which stood in the middle of a wonderful wide garden. This garden was situated on the right side of the road, after the fork of the road from the west. Around it was a high fence made of thin wood slats, through which it was possible to see everything that went on in the garden.

The gate of the garden was open all day long, but no one ever could put even his foot inside because next to the gate, for guarding purposes, lay two large dogs, ready to devour anyone who dared pass through the gate without permission.

After many years, I became friends with these two dogs (and I do not remember if they were the same dogs or others), and they even allowed me to pat their backs. I did not have much faith in them and I avoided staying alone in their company .... but more about this later.

Across from the high iron gate, in the depths of the garden, it was possible to see 'their Excellencies'' palace, and its long rows of thick tall pillars, whose whiteness blinded the eyes.

From the gate to the main entrance of the palace stretched a wide pathway, covered in yellow brick and bordered on both sides by rows of flowers of all kinds and colors, whose pleasant and pungent smell made one drunk with their perfume. To the right and left of the gate stretched rows of large, broad trees, whose branches wove together to make a tangled canopy like that of a Sukkah.

The broad paths intersected, in the depths of the garden, with many other narrower paths, which were always silent. No one had ever seen a human tread those paths, and apparently no one ever got to enjoy their deep silence.

I well remember that in the days of our childhood, a group of us children would, during the hot summer hours, leave our dusty and heat-prostrated village, in which there were no trees or greenery, and hike 'out of town' in order to breath some cool and refreshing air. It was then that in our childish hearts awoke a deep sense of jealousy to see the quiet, wonderful, secret-filled, and yet empty garden where no one ever saw a living soul. Unconsciously, it penetrated into our childish minds that something was wrong here: this world order did not fit moral ethical and humanistic principles. From this sprang the thought: here stands a cramped village, squeezed in between two rivers without any room to grow and expand beyond its boundaries, just as it does not have any air to freely breathe. And right beside it, a few steps away, sat such a big garden, beautiful and large, whose air is cool, refreshing and healthful, just as if it were a corner of the Garden of Eden. But no one gets any use or enjoyment from it because no one has permission to go inside and enjoy its goodness.

For twelve or thirteen year old boys, as we were then, these feelings of jealousy and this way of thinking was natural. But none of us imagined the possibility and the need to change this world order.

But all across Russia, people older that us had already thought about this. They dreamed about the realization of the thoughts that ran around in chaos in our childish minds and seemed to us impossible and unrealistic. They thought about the opening of all the locked and fenced gardens, into which everyone could enter without regard to social status. They took upon themselves to change the fixed order of the world which had always existed, and to form a 'Garden of

Eden' for every man in our sinful and rotten world. Years later, at the time of the October Revolution in Russia, when it was thought that here, this beautiful dream was about to be realized, when they actually opened wide all the locked palaces and their fenced gardens and set them aside for the use of all the citizens, then also from our village did they chase the guard dogs in the Nobles' 'Court' and destroyed the garden fence that had been fenced off for generations. Then it was possible to hope that now we as well, the Jews of the village, would be able to enjoy it, but then they beset our village, and all the villages and towns of Israel, in all the empire of Russia - with a sea of sorrows, torments, punishments and acts of terror, that suppressed the desire to enjoy the Garden of the Nobles and endangered life itself. But on this I will write in a special chapter.

For the sake of honesty, I must mention that even then, when entrance to the garden was forbidden to us, we enjoyed it greatly. If not from the garden and its fresh air, then our enjoyment came when we tasted its wonderful apples and pears that grew in its groves, in one of the corners of the large garden itself.

This grove was held in tenancy over many years by a villager, Moshe Tzvias (Moshe of Tzviah) who sold its fruits in the market. Those were real fruits! When one's teeth penetrated the flesh of such a 'noble' apple, two streams of juice flowed from both sides of the mouth. When one did not want the juice to go to waste one sucked it, you will excuse me, from the apple itself: and such was the fate of the wonderful 'noble' pears, as well.

It goes without saying that such 'sucking' was not particularly modern, and it can be understood that it was also not aesthetic (pleasant though it was.) How can one understand sucking or sipping from an apple or a pear? One sips soup or fish chowder after one has tired from dipping in it the soft absorbent challah. But apples and pears - all the world knows that their way is to be chewed and eaten. But we had no other choice - either to suck and feel the wonderful taste, or to throw them away and get rid of them. Because of this we did not think much about it and did not check if it was nice or not, aesthetic or not .... and we sucked them.

During the summer, when the fruit began to ripen, Moshe Tzvias would completely move into the garden. In it he would set up his big Sukkah and stay and enjoy himself in the garden day and night until he had gathered the last fruit from the latest-ripening trees.

Until the first fruits began to ripen, Moshe Tzvias did not sit on his hands. He would walk through the large, wide grove and gather from under the trees the green fruits that had been blown down by the strong winds. This green fruit was not edible, but if it was cooked in a small amount of sugar, its taste was ambrosial and it made an excellent compote.

He would distribute these fruits among the Jewish tradeswomen in the garden, who would fill great wooden baskets and sell them, immediately, to the women of the village. The value of these fruits grew in the days approaching the Sabbath. One such 'measure' (they sold them in large wooden measures) could be bought for six Prutot (one and a half American cents) and every housewife purchased such a 'healthy bargain.'

It also happened that because of these 'healthy bargains' a panic broke out in our village and caused great fear among the tradeswomen in the market. When Moshe Tzvias distributed the green windfalls to the tradeswomen, they would sit in the market streets and fill their great wooden baskets, ready to serve their customers - the housewives milling around them. At this festive moment, as if from out of the earth, emerged Michalko Stoski the policeman. In one hand he held his long thick nightstick and in the other he held an object which he kept concealed under his coat (it would soon be known what this secret object was.) He made his way to one of the tradeswomen who sat in the midst of a group of women who were frightened to the depths of their souls by the threatening stance of this large and clumsy figure. They immediately moved aside and cleared the way for him to stand face to face with the tradeswomen and their baskets filled with 'healthy bargains.' Michalko Stoski lifted up his thick nightstick and set his face in a serious expression befitting a member of the police force. He would deliver an announcement and declaration in a declamation that thundered in his bass voice and spread not only through the length and breadth of the market, but also through all the surrounding streets and alleys.

"Slochyata gospondini!" ("Listen, housewives!" He gave his speech in Ukrainian.) "In the name of the lord the Urdanik, the Pristav and also 'Yabo vilitsistavo' the Isperavnik (ranks of bureaucrats in the Czar's regime), and so on, up to the Czar Batshoshka ('father Czar') who I am not worthy to mention, I announce to you, tradeswomen, that such 'filth' that you see in the baskets is forbidden, by law, for sale. And when you fill your stomachs with it, it is possible, God forbid, to get, what is called, the real cholera, and according to the Urdanik, this cholera is liable to spread and infect our mother Russia and reach even up to the Czar Batshoshka and infect even him with the cholera. So says the Lord Urdanik, not I, and because of this I have a most serious order, that as soon as I see such 'filth' in the marketplace, I must empty them from the baskets, crush them with my boots and I mean to do so." At the end of this long speech that was heard in the shaking ears of all the tradeswomen and all the other women who stood around them, Michalko Stoski immediately placed his thick nightstick under his arm. In one hand he grabbed the basket full of 'healthy bargains' and swiftly tossed its contents onto the ground. With his other hand he took from underneath his coat a large bottle full of carbolic and poured it over the green fruit rolling on the ground. After this, he added "Here's what I will do," and repeated once more his previous remarks. After he had completed his important mission, which had taken but the blink of an eye, Michalko vanished, as if the earth had swallowed him up. One can imagine the panic and tumult that broke out among the women who were there in the market among the tradeswomen. The unfortunate housewives had to run away from there with their empty baskets, without having purchased their 'healthy bargains' for their Sabbath compote. Despite this, they could find a solution and get for themselves, with God's help, from David Schindel-Pitches or Esther the Spinster, some plums or pears - dried - from which they could make a good and pleasant compote, and when some raisins are added to it, it is food fit for kings, and the whole body enjoys it. It is, of course, a little more expensive, but it is a good thing to have for the Sabbath. This way, no one would, heaven forbid, be without tzimmes for the Sabbath.

In the market, not a trace of the tradeswomen remained. They caught up their baskets full of 'treife' goods and went off into the neighboring alleyways, where they were sure that the 'savage hand' of Michalko would not reach them. Thus they prevented sure loss and damage to themselves. In the marketplace itself remained only the stench of the carbolic that was spilled and the tradeswoman who had suffered the loss. She sat on her stool and cursed her bitter fate.

It so happened that the 'punishing hand' of Michalko Stoski fell on the head of the widow of Aharon-Yaakov, the shoemaker, who was also the 'new victim.' Thus sat Aharon-Yaakovka crying by herself in the market, keening and listing her woes, as was her way, to the Master of the Universe. And her complaints were truly justified and logical:

"It was enough," she claimed, "that you took from me, my Lord, my good treasure, Aharon-Yaakov; you did this with your holy hand, and at any rate, he was already a 'broken dish' and I did not get much use, anyway, from him. When you brought down fire from the skies, on that same terrible Friday morning, and burned my small meager house, and I with my small orphans, were left homeless, I accepted also this as a punishment that I deserved. Despite this, when you hit me with one hand, verily with the other hand you did to us great kindness, and you showed us a great miracle, because we did not lose much in the fire, me and my homeless orphans. All these sorrows I accept and apparently I was worthy of them. But that I should be punished by the hand of that coarse boor and his piggish kind, by the hand of that despised drunk Michalko Stoski? Punishment like this I did not deserve."

After all her complaints against the Master of the Universe, Aharon-Yaakovka once again became agitated and once more took up her crying and howling in the highest tones and all the alleyways in the area were filled with them. People who saw this behavior as a regular occurrence smiled to hear her complaints and howls. The howling came also to the ears of Moshe-Tzvias who was in his grove. He took them, in his earthy simplicity, in the quietest manner. From the grove he sent her by special messenger words of joking condolence and a healthy portion of admonishment. He instructed the messenger to say to her thus:

"What's with you that you complain with your howling to the Creator? One might think, who knows how much this damage cost? I know that all the damage does not amount to more than one ruble, which you have not yet paid to me, and if you ask it of me, I will be willing to write it off, thus you have already escaped all damages. Why do you mix up the loss from today with all your previous troubles, which are not at all troubles, but blessings and salvation? All of us know that your Aharon-Yaakov, the shlemiel, with his walleyes, was, in his last years, a 'man cut down,' a wasted man, worthless, who wasn't able to make even a simple patch on a shoe. Anyway, you had to sit in the market with your baskets, to support your children and save some pennies for medicines for your Aharon-Yaakov, which helped him like 'wind cups for the dead' [a Yiddish expression] and finally he went to his reward. You should have accepted all this as the wisdom of the Blessed Be His Name, to let your Yaakov sleep in peace in his final resting place and not disturb him over every little thing. And why do you wail about your 'palace' with its straw roof, that went up on that same Friday, from heavenly fire, when all the villagers know that it was nothing but a hovel that was liable to collapse any day on you and on your children, large and small, and to kill all of you, that there in the world of truth, Aharon-Yaakov could not help you. Because of this, stop your empty wailing, leave your insignificant and exaggerated troubles and your empty baskets, and go home to your house and your children to sleep and rest. Tomorrow, G-d willing, I will gather such fruit that no one has ever seen. It will shine and glow in all the market and you will be able to put that coarse man, Michalko Stoski, with all his orders, deep into the earth. If everything I said today does not come to pass tomorrow in entirety, my name will no longer be Moshe Tzvias."

The words of condolence, and the promise of Moshe Tzvias, were delivered to Aharon Yaakovka by the messenger, word for word. They strengthened her and lifted her spirits. She knew that Moshe Tzvias' promise would certainly be kept. What he says, he does; what he decrees, he makes good. She left the empty market in the late afternoon. With the empty baskets in her hands and not a coin in her pockets, she returned to her home. Moshe Tzvias had made his promise and the matter was not particularly difficult for him. The 'green windfalls' he gave away almost for free, and from this he made a rather good profit without even taking into account the landlord's crop estimate.

Apples and pears of the first quality ripened on the trees. It was possible for him to gather from these large amounts of excellent fruit and bring them to market but first and foremost he took care to supply to Aharon Yaakovka the choicest fruits and thus keep his promise so that even she would profit after her pain of today's damage - this Moshe Tzvias thought to himself. even though all the damage was at his own expense, he would not lose anything from it. It would be as if the 'alley thieves' had stolen the apples and pears. Moshe Tzvias did not shake the trees to take off the fruit; he would pluck them with his hands with extreme care, each apple and pear, and prepare a great quantity of fruit for the next day.

The afternoon of the following day, glowing in the shopkeepers baskets, were large yellow pears, with long thin necks, which spread a pleasant scent afar. Next to them sparkled large, shiny apples, a little pale, but with blushing cheeks, a sign that they were ready to eat. They looked as if they begged to be tasted and blessed with the 'shechechiyanu' blessing.

The housewives circled around the baskets, filled with wonder at the marvelous fruits, undecided as to what to do. If they were to prepare compote from these it would cost too much but to serve as refreshment for the Sabbath afternoon - there could not be anything better.

Every housewife bought a certain amount of the fruit according to her means. The tradeswomen were in an elevated mood. They received excellent merchandise for sale and in everyone's opinion it was very tasty.

Aharon Yaakovka forgot her crisis of the day before. She sat, encouraged, next to her full baskets and was filled with a whim. She desired that Michalko Stoski would appear up now in the market, see with his murderous eyes all that was taking place here, and he, astounded, would for sure want to gobble from the baskets. But she wished him ill. That's what he deserved for his 'good deeds' yesterday.

Both the tradeswomen and the housewives were satisfied. The only one who was unhappy was Moshe Tzvias. He walked around the large grove, looked at the trees laden with the fruits that had ripened early, and suddenly many thoughts entered his head. Unnatural things are happening here this year, he thought. He had known this orchard for many years. He knew its nature, the value and yield of each tree, just as he knew his own children. When the trees finished their flowering he already knew how many apples or pears each tree would produce, without taking into account, at the time of reckoning, the damaged trees that gave poor yields.

Now he noticed to his amazement that each of the 'sterile ones' that had all the years thought to be barren, this year put out a rich and heavy crop. This wonder he was not able to comprehend in any way in his simple mind. Aside from this, he noticed another thing that confused even his senses and laid to waste all his experience and all his calculations over many years.

The old and experienced orchard master knew that the first fruits to ripen were the fruits of the trees that grew on the fringes of the garden, those that were exposed to the heat and light of the sun. After this came the turn of the trees within the garden and only at the end did those that stood at its center and in the shade ripen completely. Thus Moshe Tzvias was able to perform his work in stages, completely and adeptly, without getting tired.

At the beginning, he cleared the green windfalls from the orchard. And even though they had received the judgement that Michalko Stoski had passed upon them, according to his "orders from above," he nevertheless succeeded in distributing them among the tradeswoman who in secrecy and with discretion gave them to the housewives. Big profits were not to be had from them but the 'garbage' (as he called them) he did not take into account anyway. Thus, any amount he received, he took as clear profit. After this he begins to deal with the first-ripening fruits. He plucks, with great care, each apple and each pear, so that he will not cause any damage to the fruit. During his labors he already manages to make an exact accounting and to decide which he will sell now and how much he must gather to save in the cool cellar and take out for next fall when fresh fruit is not to be found at all. Then he could take out his apples and pears, well preserved, and get the best price.

It should be noted that a simple man and a man of the people such as Moshe Tzvias never in his life studied economics and did not have any idea about the laws of supply and demand, yet he understood and felt with his professional sense, that it was worthwhile taking less fruit to market, so as not to supply it with an excess of merchandise causing the prices to drop - a situation which would cause him losses.

If the fruit had ripened gradually, Moshe Tzvias would do his work without hurrying and would have enough time to carry out his plan completely. He would be able to supply enough fruit to market and also, most importantly, to take care that the most beautiful apples and pears would 'go to sleep' in the cellar.

When could he realize and carry out all the plans that he had make ahead of time? When everything went as it should. That was the way things went during all the years he had held the farm in tenancy. This year strange miracles had happened which he truly saw as a 'disaster.' Because how would he be able to manage with an abundance of ripe fruit, without the evil eye, which one cannot leave even one more day on the trees if one does not want it to go to waste?

Moshe Tzvias continues to ponder his thoughts: even if he calls forth and engages in labor all his family members and the sons of Tzviah and her grandchildren, would they be able to deal with all this abundance, within a few days, without leaving them to stay an excessive amount of time on the trees to rot and be destroyed entirely? (We are talking about real manual labor because he had no other way to pick fruit.)

If this disaster had happened to another man, he would have already found a solution to this serious question and there would have been no more place for problems. If the Master of the Universe, blessed him with such excess and everything had already ripened, why pick by hand? Are apples not like etrogs, for example, that one must pick them one by one and take care that they not be defaced, G-d forbid? With a healthy shake of the tree or specific branches, it is possible in a few moments to remove all the fruit and so to finish tree after tree until the end of the harvest. Afterwards there is nothing left to do except fill large containers with the fruit, take them down to the airy cellar, spread them on a bed of straw and finish with the matter. Now, orchard, it has been a nice experience, see you next year.

This is what every orchard man would do it such a disaster happened to him. But what of our Moshe Tzvias? He is not one of these who can agree to adopt such coarse methods with something as delicate as fresh and juicy fruit. He, who all the days of his life (during the seasons) spent in orchards, looked upon the flowering of the trees and the slow dropping of the blooms when one begins to see the tiny bud of an apple and pear. These buds start to grow more and more. They also change their color, at first dark green, after this light green and afterwards from light green they turn to light yellowish and then the yellow starts, at the end of everything to turn to light red and dark red. Following the start of the growth of the fruit, a sense of fatherhood took root in him. He sees the fruit as a living thing and feels a need to relate to it with care and delicacy, he who was enmeshed in it all his life, pointed out frequently that if the fruit was good (and he only spoke of good fruit because in his eyes other fruit had no value) one must take more care with in than with a baby because - he would continue explaining with a parable - a child who falls and receives a bruise, no danger awaits him. The wound will heal and the boy will stay whole as if nothing special had happened. He will continue to grow and will become, within time, a whole man. Good fruits, like a pear or an apple, when they receive a bruise, even the smallest, then woe unto them. It is as if it were just a light touch on the outer peel but you can be sure that under the peel, a light wound has started to develop, and this wound emits a pus that spreads within and causes the entire fruit to rot. With fruit such as this, it is good to take it immediately to the market and sell it, even if 'half for free.' But to send it to the cellar to sleep and to keep it for the times of better prices - it is impossible! There will be nothing left to sell because all will be rotten. This was the thought and concern of Moshe Tzvias for the fruit. Because of this it was no wonder that on that same day he paced inside the grove confused and in a black mood. He looked at the unexpected abundant harvest with which he was blessed that year without being able to think of ideas as to what to do. He went around the length and breadth of the garden and suddenly his mind was filled with the desire to remember whether in earlier years such a thing had happened and how he had handled it then. While he strode, full of thought, Moshe Tzvias, without realizing it, left the garden and stood next to the tall fence at the end of the wide road.

At moments like these, his feet drove him like a car without purpose and without awareness. Then he saw the youths, carefree, who came out in the summer twilight, group after group from the narrow dust-filled village, to breath the cool and refreshing air and passed by the Noble's garden. Looking at the young hikers occupied old Moshe Tzvias's mind and he forgot, for the blink of an eye, his worries and what was going on in his bitter heart.

That same late twilight, we, three friends, met him as he leaned against the fence. It was already dark but we saw the sorrow in his tall, lean form, that pondered in the dark behind the thin fence. This trio was composed of my closest friend Isaac Bierish, of blessed memory, who died afterwards at a young age. My second friend, David Fritz, who did not succeed in emigrating (as he wanted to do) and was no doubt murder during the extermination of the Jewish towns and villages. The writer of these lines, whose luck was with him, managed to leave, at a later time, the village of his birth and emigrate to far away and hospitable Argentine. Thus he was able to reach out, via these modest lines, to memorialize the recollections of his village of birth, Yampol, and the memories of all his dear ones and loved ones of Yampol, who went up in the conflagration and were exterminated during the last destruction.

The three of us stopped exactly opposite Moshe Tzvias, with the deep canal in front of us separating the garden and the main road and serving as a barrier between him and us. He, perhaps, did not see us, buried deep in the worries that busied his mind, and was not able to recognize all of those who stood in front of him in the dark, at a distance of four or five meters. We all shouted to him from afar, with one voice, "Good evening to you, Reb Moshe!" Apparently he recognized our voices and was pleasantly surprised by our unexpected greeting because his mood changed for the better. "Happy New Year to you, children!" Moshe Tzvias immediately answered in his soft voice, happy at the opportunity to forget his worries and talk with someone.

He called to us again: "Are you going to look for some fresh air, children, as it looks suffocating in the village?" "Yes, yes, Reb Moshe! You hit the nail on the head," we answered him. "Because of this we left the village. It is good for you all, Reb Moshe, for you and your family to spend day and night in your grove in its cool, healthy and refreshing air. It will bring you longer lives, until one hundred and twenty years."

From afar we heard a deep sigh. Apparently he remembered once again his earlier worries and given the opportunity, was about to speak about what was in his heart and gain some relief. However he immediately changed his mind, thinking that youths would not understand much about delicate matters and we could not give him any good advice. Because of this he turned the conversation in another direction and loudly called to us saying: "Would you children like to revive your spirits with a juicy apple or pear that was picked at this moment?"

This question caught us by surprise and we saw that the good Moshe Tzvias wanted to take advantage of the opportunity given to him and give us pleasure from his abundant yield. We peeked inside and saw, even though it was dark, that he wanted us to receive from his hands a tasty juicy fruit but we were unsure whether it was proper for us, important children of well-to-do householders, to take something for nothing. We were certain that he meant to give it to us as a gift.

"Yes, yes, Reb Moshe!" we answered him. "We would be happy to receive from you something to lift our spirits but only on condition that you will accept payment and that it will not be a gift." In order to show him that we had good intention we added "We thank you very much for your attention, Reb Moshe, but if you want to give us pleasure, you must agree to receive from us at least a symbolic payment, otherwise we cannot accept."

The good and straightforward Reb Moshe immediately understood that by forcing us he would not be able to work out anything with the proud children of well-to-do householders. Because of this he shouted to us in a discouraged voice, "Do whatever you wish, children!"

We wrapped a Russian silver coin in white paper, tied it to a medium size rock and threw it over the high fence in the direction of Moshe Tzvias. He caught it with great dexterity and disappeared with it into the darkness of the garden, shouting to us, "I will return immediately, children."

Not much time passed and once again we saw the tall form of Moshe Tzvias between the crowded trees, carrying a large basket full of apples and pears. As he stopped across from us he breathed heavily and began to toss us perfect apples and pears calling "Catch them, children."

We were astonished at the goodness of his wonderful heart and we did not have much time to think because the juicy apples and pears flew continuously towards us and we had to catch them in flight. We filled all our pockets and hands with them and Moshe Tzvias did not stop tossing them at us; his mission was not finished and it was as if a blessing had entered his basket.

We shouted to him: "Reb Moshe, in the name of G-d, it is enough, we have nowhere to put the fruit. He answered "Catch them, catch them, children, and here is another one. With G-d's help, I have enough like this."

With this, the biggest surprise awaited us because with the last of the apples and pears, he also tossed back the stone to which had been tied the wrapped silver coin. He did this with great agility and we only managed to hear his last words: "Eat in good health, good night to you, children!" and he immediately disappeared into the darkness of the garden.

We stood embarrassed because we had thought ourselves to be intelligent but came to realize that the simple Moshe Tzvias had surpassed us with his wisdom and intelligence. We recognized and were impressed by his 'quick uptake' thanks to which he could carry out his good intentions and treat us against our will.

Already, over half a century has passed since that summer evening, and still, before my eyes, stands the figure of the elderly kind Moshe Tzvias, as if he were still among the living, his loving words still ring in my ears: "Eat in good health, children!"

I still feel the taste of the wonderful juicy apples and pears with which he treated us, against our will, that same unforgettable evening, in such a human and humble manner.

It would be unjust of me if, after having dedicated so much attention to him, I did not mention, in even a few works, his Polish woman, Feyge, who was his 'helpmate.' She was also called Feyge Moshe Tzvias and she truly deserved that honorable title because aside from her being a 'woman of valor' and a wonderful 'creation,' she also was a 'Cossack Jewess.' It was said that she had a mouth of nails and that it was better to cry "uncle" than fall afoul of her mouth. But this is a slight exaggeration.

The truth was that she was a wise and intelligent woman who never allowed herself to be put down and always knew what was happening. In contrast to this her quiet husband, Moshe Tzvias, was an innocent lamb. Because of this she did not agree with his dealings and always ran her own business.

As a tenant, for many years, she ran the dairies of the 'noble' manors surrounding the village and supplied the villagers with milk, butter, cheese, cream and all the other dairy products. Top do this work she enlisted 'with a strong arm' all her numerous family members and even her Moshe had to answer to her after the season of the fruit and orchard.

The brother of Moshe, Mordechai Tzvias, tenanted like his brother, gardens of fruit and groves and also dealt in beekeeping. He would buy many hives from the 'nobles' and produce honey and wax. It was known that this business did not cause him any financial losses.

All of Tzviah's sons were straightforward men, fair, plain and hard-working. There were many of them in the village.

As luck had it, the majority of their family succeeded in leaving our village before the first World War and after it and emigrated to what was then far-off America. But they did not neglect the commandment to "be fruitful and multiply" and the same thing happened there as in our village, their numbers greatly increased. If there, in America, they had been successful in settling not only in one city, but in one neighborhood or perhaps one street, they would have had the possibility and right of calling it 'Yampol Street.' In this way they would have memorialized the name of the village of Yampol, which was uprooted and destroyed, and would never have allowed her to be forgotten.

THE FIRST YIZKOR OF THE LAST TIME
by David Rubin

[79]

When Fate decreed that we should flee, we fled without knowing to where. Late in the evening, we reached the town of Yampol naked, barefoot, hungry and thirsty, tired and exhausted, and accompanied by the bombs of the gangster pilots.

It was dark, with no sign of life, not a candle was alight. As if everything was dead. The houses seemed wrapped in black, the sky was covered with thick black clouds. The black of the buildings merged with the darkness outside.

I'm lost. I have no idea where I am.

A piercing rain whips our faces. A biting wind rages and magnifies the ferocity of the rain. There is nowhere to shelter.

The air carries the echoes of exploding bombs. From close by we hear the voices of barking dogs and mewling cats in their wild choruses.

My home town! I have lived with you for two-thirds of my life! Every one of your alleys, your houses and your corners is engraved on my memory and I see it all as if in the palm of my hand. Now I stand in despair, lost and bewildered ... carefully, like a blind man stretching out his searching hands in front of him I feel a wall and find a window. Quietly I knock on it. But all is silent, all is still, all is dead.

As I knock louder, I hear the whispered voice of someone saying, "Hush, my child", and the words are accompanied by a barely heard question: "Kto tam?" ("Who is there?" in Russian.)

"David Ester from Kremenetz. I can't find my home, where I have lived for forty years. I beg you, show me the way to Hirschel from the wall, or to Feivel Shloms, who lives in my house."

"My husband is at the front, I am on my own with the children. They will scream if I leave them along in the dark, which is not a good idea just now ... but" she continued "at the end of the wall, at the corner, turn right. Carry straight on and you will soon come to Feivel Shloms."

There I met all my relatives. They had all gathered as if they felt something awful and terrifying, and as if they knew that the hours together were numbered.

Who can describe such a meeting? We embraced each other with kisses and tears. Could I describe all that?

A whole family met together. A whole family wept silently on that last dark night. Before the dark miserable day they touched each other's hearts.

The next morning, everyone in the town knew of our arrival and without thought of the fierce and hostile bombardment, friends, comrades and acquaintances arrived. The sadness on their faces told what was happening inside them ... of their despair, their hopelessness and their broken and depressed spirits.

Their reception, their greetings, "Hello, how are you Dovid?" were so pitiful and full of despair that the heart broke with sorrow at the sight.

"So Dovid, you are fleeing. Where to? Do you know anyone there? Haven't you thought of what will happen to you there? The chaos is widespread and who knows whether 'they' will catch you there?"

I replied that I did not want my family to meet the German murderers face to face. I advised them also to leave everything and to save their families.

Their response? They already knew the worth of 'the refuge in the east,' that it was all the same whether it was the SS or the NKVD.

When I recall their appearance, their despair, their neglect and their depression, which were expressed in their conversation, their reasoning, their unjustified response and their mistaken and illogical obstinacy, I would be made of steel if my heart did not break from pain and sorrow.

Yes! All my nearest and dearest took on too great a danger. But does anyone have the right to judge them according to the tragedy which befell them? After all, it could have been different. Those who were destroyed could have been the ones to write such a memoir of us the 'clever' ones who were saved.

THE FUNERAL AND THE ESCORT

My friends and relatives from Yampol accompanied us with spontaneous bitter tears, with spasmodic wailing, with ululations and with hysterical screaming.

Women stood at the doors of their homes. They wiped their tears with their aprons and shouted after us: "Dovid! Hava! Dear friends! Go in happiness! May G-d give you all good things and help us to meet again."

Only some of the blessings were fulfilled. With G-d's help we stayed alive but to our great sorrow we never again saw our friends and never again met our relatives.

A pure and holy community. More than one thousand Jews, all of them precious, holy, honest, hard-working, good-hearted, charitable and learned, were destroyed together with their children, infants and babies. The town of Yampol was completely demolished, together with all of its antiquities.

There is no remnant of the magnificent synagogue, that was the glory of the town. All was destroyed and burnt by the German criminals.

Who will lament you? For there is no-one left who will weep a tear for you! Woe to us all! Wretched, wretched! Who will lament you?

(Translated from Yiddish [into Hebrew] by A.Z. Tarshish)

REB ZALMAN THE POOR
(An example of a repentant sinner in Yampol)
by Dr. Yitzchak Weissstaub

[82]

Some call him 'hidden' and others called him a 'repentant sinner' but he himself said that his name was Zalman the Poor. It is still not known where he was from. He lived in our town for thirty years or more. When he was occasionally asked where he was from, he would reply with a soft affectionate laugh: "Idiots! Why are you bothering your brains about where I come from, it would be better to ask where I am going!" And when he was asked where he was headed, he would reply that he did not know because it did not depend on his will and desire ... he never wore new clothes, to this day he still wears only the clothes in which he came to us thirty years ago. Of course, they are by now covered with patches on the patches so that it is no longer possible to discern the original fabric. He was always busy mending them; as soon as he mended them in one place, there would be a fresh tear somewhere else, and so on ...

It was said of him that he wanted to live in our town because of its ancient cemetery and they said that early every morning, summer and winter, he would visit it, stand outside the fence, examine it from every angle, mutter a few indecipherable words secretly between his teeth and return to town. He lived in a small room in the cloister of the Ostra Chassidim and he was very happy with it. More than once town notables had offered him somewhere to sleep and keep his belongings but he was stubborn, always refused, because there he was free, his own master, no one looked at him suspiciously or as he said 'with a sideways glance' and he lived independently...

He made a living partly from old rags, second-hand clothes, which he picked up casually while walking along the road and sometimes by looking through rubbish tips and courtyards and partly by begging during certain periods. For a long time people in the town thought him an uncouth person who only knew how to pray with difficulty, without understanding the words, but they later found out that they were mistaken for he was discovered late one night in a hidden corner with a candle burning and a big Gemarra open in front of him. He was so immersed in deep study that he did not notice that someone had opened the door and come in. If he was ever asked the name of his father he would lose his temper and get very angry, almost coming to blows. Even when he was occasionally called up to read from the Torah and asked his father's name he would shrink and not answer...

In front of the cloister where he lived, the square was empty and clean and you couldn't find a speck of dust or the smallest bit of rubbish. The ground around was carpeted with a floor of pebbles which he had laid with his own hands. It was an amazing sight to see him lying on the floor at this pleasant task. A many-colored kippa, which the town wags called a badger or Turkish hat, would be on his head and he would be lying at full length on the ground working earnestly like a craftsman. If someone met him while he was at this agreeable work and asked him: "Reb Zalman! What are you doing? Why are you wasting your feeble energy?" he would reply with a slight giggle of bitter mockery: "I am going to bequeath this to the town for the future generations, these hard, cold stones on the eternal earth. Perhaps someone will remember me on Pesach eve when clearing out the dirt," and carried on working.

The birds were his children. Every day at dawn he would stand outside the synagogue with his hands full of breadcrumbs and seeds and a huge flock of all sorts of birds would surround him. With a joyful cry of "Tweet! Tweet!" they would snatch the crumbs and seeds from his hands. It is no exaggeration to say that they considered him their father: they sat on his shoulder, flew to his hands and knew with absolute certainty that, under his protection, they would come to no harm. He knew the character of each one of the guests at his table, their good and bad points, their natural inclinations to the finest detail; and according to how he understood their nature, he would call each one by their fitting name; this one was called Cheeky, another Speedy, Ganef, Humble, Snooty, Simpleton - the one who cannot ask questions, and each name was accurate in its sensitive understanding which he had acquired through experience.

He loved little children very much and was particularly affectionate to poor orphans whose mothers had died while they were still babies and who had never known a mother's warm embrace nor heard a mother's pleasant words of comfort. He sometimes brought them toys and played with them, washed their filthy hair and occasionally cured their boils with various remedies, herbs and charms.

He loved to listen and hear the soft, clear, sorrowful voice of a youth studying a problem in Gemarra with his Rabbi and in particular before Pesach, he loved the original tune of the Song of Songs as sung by the school children. When he heard this, his eyes filled with tears and he had such pleasant daydreams ... at this time he would visit the cheders of our town daily, to hear the Song of Songs.

The Haskalah [Enlightenment] followed him to our town. Our town is very isolated and has little connection with the central towns; it was shrouded in the medieval darkness. We did not know that the world had other kingdoms, languages, experiences and in general terrible deeds and events waiting to be born, to fill the universe. But because of him, our eyes were opened. The sun of enlightenment shone down to our earth from the skies; in his bag were found some crumpled pages of Ha-Maggid and these were a great excitement for the college students, hungry to know everything. Because of him they grew wings to fly wherever the wind carried them, or as is said, 'they fell into bad ways.' He influenced a wealthy youth to sign up for Ha-Tzfira and he encouraged the youngsters to read it and explained politics to them and with keen logic he analyzed the political issues engaging the wide world. He was particularly interested in the Dreyfus trial. He waited impatiently for each day's edition of Ha-Tzfira. It got so far that he promised us that when Dreyfus would receive justice and be released from Devil's Island he would throw away his patched clothes and try to make some new ones.

He liked to relate his enthralling anecdotes about what he had seen and heard in the days of his travels in various cities to his young friends in the cloister. Particularly on cloudy days, when nature was angry, we would gather around him and he would open up the hidden treasury of his memories to us and reveal secrets to us, mysteries, amazing things that stirred the imagination while we listened attentively and with curiosity to every word and syllable which he uttered. There was a thread of grace, poetry and glory running through all his anecdotes; in his longing to tell stories, he added various comments, summarized what we could learn from them, seasoned them with popular sayings and ultimately would always finish with an ethical idea as a general conclusion to the whole matter. The 'repentant sinner' felt a certain wonderful spiritual enjoyment in telling his anecdotes to an audience, or to use his words, 'a sort of huge internal impulse to tell' ... so that he often did not notice that he had told them more than once or twice before so that we knew them by heart in every detail and would sometimes correct him if he told it differently from the way he had told us previously.

A stranger once came to our town. The 'repentant sinner' greatly honored him and served him and the attitude was mutual between them so that the stranger once whispered a request to him to reveal the mysteries of the world, the coming of the Messiah ... a great laugh then burst from his mouth and he said that, with respect, he was only a beggar, not one of the Thirty-six Righteous ...

I saw him for the last time after eight years absence. He was still in his small room in the Ostra cloister, but Oh! how his appearance had altered, his expression and even more his spirit! His cheeks were sunken, there were broad and deep wrinkles on his big white brow. His big eyes sunk in their orbits were misty and bleary, with no movement or twitch as if they had frozen in their sockets. The mocking chuckle which had been on his lips and which had always accompanied him through his hard life had disappeared. His head was no longer held erect. He did not exchange even a single word with anyone; he had become silent. Some said that the disturbances in Russia had affected him badly, and depressed him. Some said that old age itself, from which there was no escape and which did not show favor to anybody, had left its heavy stamp on him. But those close to him, who knew his secrets, said that he had once opened his heart to them after repeated entreaties, and explained to them the reason for the huge changes in his spirit.

A crow with a crooked beak had been his downfall. For fifteen years he had been feeding a crow with a crooked beak every winter. One harsh winter he had been walking along the street in the morning, minding his own business. There was heavy frost over the ground, everyone was frozen stiff and suddenly a crow with a bent beak was flying along sadly croaking "Caw! Caw!" even though despite the snow, under the rubbish, there was something to slightly ease his oppressive hunger. But the other crows were beating him to it because they had straight beaks. The 'Repentant Sinner' noticed this, pitied the crow, approached him with love and fed him. When the spring came, he flew off to the fields to find food and in winter he would come back to him in the town to be fed. Fifteen years had passed this way but in the sixteenth year the crow had not returned ... The 'Repentant Sinner' saw in this an omen of a bad future, a dark prophecy of evil awaiting to befall him. This caused him to fall into a depression and terrible sadness. He withdrew from people, isolated himself in the forest and prepared himself for the day of his death which he thought was already breathing down his neck. From then, he had degenerated day by day. He wandered around like a shadow and however hard his friends tried to speak to his heart, to prove with conclusive signs and wonders that this was merely the fault of his deceitful imagination, total folly and nothing bad was about to happen - none of this helped.

Editorial Comment

The sketch of Reb Zalman the Poor was written by the late Dr. Yitzchak Weisstaub, the son of Rabbi Eliyahu Ziegermeister of Yampol. 'Reb Zalman the Poor' was a unique and mysterious character, or as many thought, genuinely one of the Thirty-Six Righteous. Not even any of the oldest townspeople knew who he was or when he had come to our town. He spent most of his time with the sick and the wretched poor, helping to find medicine for them. On the day that Dreyfus was freed, he kept his vow and danced in front of the synagogue in the presence of all the worshippers. He did not want to eat at other people's expense and only on Shabbath was he a permanent guest of Rabbi Netanel Horzshach, the father of the late Yaakov Horzshach.

IN MEMORIAM
(A LAMENT FOR THE MARTYRED DEAD OF VOLHYNIA)
by H.B. Ayalon

[86]

A

Out of recognition of a deep and holy spiritual duty, a fitting custom has been adopted by the survivors of majestic Jewish Volhynia living in Israel - to gather every year on the tragic and bloody date of 14th Elul, in order to recall the sacred martyrs of Volhynia, who fell into the hands of filthy and damned oppressors and murderers. This custom has taken root in most of the municipal organizations which in recent years have held their own memorial meetings in small groups of survivors of their communities. A special feeling fills the hearts of the congregants as if the pure souls of our murdered ones are hovering over our heads and filling the hall.

This communing has two aspects: as Jews, we must remember those beloved people who were distinguished by all the good Jewish attributes, whose good name went before them and was famed in the Jewish world for their great Torah scholars, their writers and poets, their Zionist and general functionaries etc: and as people from Volhynia we remember with awe and reverence our fathers and mothers, our brothers and sisters, our friends and acquaintances, the thread of whose lives was cut short in such a tragic and cruel way.

It is a hard and heavy task to mourn and eulogize a beloved one who has left us the way of all flesh; how much more so to lament those who meet an untimely and unnatural death: and how immeasurably and incomparably hard to bewail the huge and terrible holocaust which had no parallel, in the darkest periods of our bloody history, from the destruction of our country and temple to present day.

Our historic enemies, which we have never lacked, rose against us in every generation to destroy and eliminate us, and not only did they never manage to put this into practice but we were able to see their downfall - Pharoah and his troops drowned in the Red Sea, Haman and his sons were hanged on the gallows which they had prepared for Mordechai, and even during the destruction of our country for the first and second time, the Babylonians and the Romans did not destroy the Jewish people. But in our own generation, woe to us, our enemy's hand was stronger and we were caught in a trap and had this small remnant not survived we would have been as lost as Sodom and Gemorrah.

Human language is too poor to give a strong and forceful expression to the terrible disaster which suddenly came down on the heads of more than 150 Jewish communities in Volhynia.

Some 600,000 people of Volhynia were destroyed in cruel and unusual deaths, men and women, Torah scholars and philosophers, writers and poets and public functionaries, and of all these who is greater, more beloved to us than mothers and fathers, brothers and sisters, young children who had never sinned. All of them pure and holy, for whom there is no substitute and no compensation.

Our reservoir of tears is far too small to weep for the tragedy and the calamity. We have already wept many tears, we have wailed and lamented, but this is just a drop in our sea of woes, and not even if our heads were made of water and our eyes were a well of tears, would we be able to mourn enough our myriad of beloved victims who were killed and slaughtered, who were burned by fire and drowned by water, who were buried alive and tortured with all sorts of cruel and unusual deaths? Our loss is as huge as the ocean and our pain is as deep as the abyss, and words and tears cannot express the feelings of our broken hearts. There is no cure for our wound which cannot heal and there is no solace for our unbearable burden.

B

One of the wonderful phenomena of human life is that, when a man's death is before him, he is dumbfounded, as if indifferent to his great tragedy. The immensity of the shock astonishes him so much that his senses are blunted and he is struck dumb. This explains the ancient custom of hiring professional mourners to lament and try for the departed, both out of respect for the dead and to soften the hearts of the mourners which have been turned to stone.

If this happens in the case of a normal death, how much more so in this situation. In the case of individual mourning it is only natural since man's end is death and it is decreed that what is covered by the earth shall be forgotten by the heart. Particularly after the latest atrocities, it can be considered a great privilege for a man to die at an old age, amongst his people and in the bosom of his family. But the recent mass mourning is not like this when the whole Jewish people is in mourning and bereaved. Is there a calamity like our calamity and a mourning like our mourning? Even the devil himself has not yet devised the right expression to describe the full extent of the tragedy which befell us.

Where are the prophets of anger and lamentation, and where are the artists with word and brush, who are able to portray a Jewish mother thrust with her babe into the grave which she and her husband have dug, holding onto her child and covering it with her body in order to shield its shivering heart from the bitter death before they are buried alive?!

And where is the hand that could describe a community of Jews, men, women and children, lying naked on the ground and licking at the dust, a sort of living cemetery, while the abominable and filthy murderers ride over their backs on horseback, crushing their flesh and trampling on them until they breathe their last, or even worse, even death betrays them and does not rescue them from these satanic tortures?!

And if we forsook our daily work and abstained from eating and drinking, and wept day and night, could we weep enough for the souls of our gentle mothers and sisters who were defiled and murdered in front of their husbands, and the children whose heads were cut off in front of their parents? Our shock and the blunting of our senses is as great as our pain and to the same extent we need mourners and lamenters who will soften our fossilized hearts and rouse us from the oblivion and unconsciousness into which we have sunk. In this mass mourning, there is no room for amnesia, nor for any remission to our great sorrow. The visions of atrocity will remain before our eyes forever and will not let us rest. The wound will long remain open and will not heal, the mass graves will remain fresh and will make the earth over the victims dance, the voice of our brothers' and sisters' blood will not cease to shout to us from the ground and to demand vengeance and restitution. The extent of the tragedy is so great that our hearts are too small to contain our compassion and our senses are too blunt to feel it and to bear it. Therefore, we have to mourn in public bit by bit, year after year. We must continue to add our tears to the national flask of tears which is as big as the tragedy and which will not be filled until the people of Israel see its revenge and its redemption, until a righteous judge shall seize the genocidal murderers and smash them against the rock.

One of the legends from the destruction of the Temple relates that the prophet Jeremiah, the great mourner, was following the sorrowful route of the exiles from Judea. He looked down and saw that the path was full of blood and the earth was spattered with the blood of the slaughtered. He saw the footprints of babes and sucklings, bent down and kissed them with love. On his way back he saw the fingers and toes which had been chopped off and thrown into the hills. He gathered them up and caressed them, embraced them and kissed them. This was when the prophet wailed his great lamentation and said: "I will weep and wail on the hilltops and lament at the oases."

Even this consolation has been denied us. The earlier Babylonian enemy, who was famed for his cruelty, was most merciful compared to the recent satanic enemy. For Nebuchadnezzar intended only to break our land's political independence, not the physical destruction of the people. So he expelled only the leaders and granted them extensive autonomy in his country, which led after two generations to the return to Zion and the resurrection of independence, while the majority of the people remained in their land But the oppressors of our time intended to exterminate the whole people, so that we would never revive.

(C)

Even the nation which played a large part in the salvation of the remnants of our people has closed the way to the graves of our fathers with an 'Iron Curtain' if not for which we would organize a lengthy pilgrimage in order to prostrate ourselves on the huge mass graves spread across the fields, the forests and by the waysides, to roll in, lick and kiss the dust covering the souls dearer to us than anything, who were placed in agony and suffering into their graves.

Perhaps in this way the pain would be eased and the disgrace would be relieved both for us and for them. But to our sorrow and distress we are prevented from doing this. Bitter fate has decreed that no-one shall know where our beloved souls are buried and we must mourn for them from afar. And with no solace for our sick hearts, nothing is left to us except our heavy mourning and the cry of our great disaster, pouring out and mixing together with the voice of the blood of our brothers which is crying out to us from the ground.

But it is not with tears alone that we shall atone for their earth and their blood. They demand a restitution for their souls from us. And we must not forget that even the right to mourn from afar also came to us through a great miracle. As is well known, the jackboots of the enemy of humanity reached the borders of our country and there was only a step between us and the destruction of the remnants of the Jewish people in their land. But a patent miracle occurred and the filthy foot of our enemy did not succeed in treading on the holy soil of our land. Furthermore his downfall began and we gained our redemption and the resurrection of independent Israel.

We will remember and recall the martyrs of the Holocaust of 5702-3. We will not forget them.

EXTRACTS FROM THE LEDGER OF THE CHEVRA KADISHA OF YAMPOL
by Arieh Leib Gellman

[90]

(The ledger was in the possession of the Gabbai, the late Rabbi Shalom Lerner.)

A

As noted before, at my request, in 5690 (1929-30) I was sent a copy of the ledger of the Chevra Kadisha in the holy community of Yampol by the head of the town's Bet Din, Rabbi Shmuel Lerner (Olav ha-Shalom), who was killed in the recent bloody Holocaust together with all of the townspeople, holy and innocent victims, may G-d avenge their blood!

In his letter to me, on the first day of the Sidra "Hu Chiyech" of 5690, [Deut. 30, 20] he wrote the following:

".....I immediately fulfilled the request of my dear friend and transcribed the register here which was written in the hand of the gaon Rabbi Yechezkel Landau, who was rabbi and Rosh Yeshiva in the town of Yampol in the Volhyn district before moving to the city of Prague. Those who thought and claimed that he was rabbi of Yampol in the district of Podolya are making a grave error. There is a tradition among the elders of this city that when the previous rabbi of Prague was on his death bed, and the residents of that city entreated him to tell them who to appoint to take his place after his death, and who could "fit that cloak," his answer was "perhaps Rabbi Meir [is right]." No one understood his reply, and they did not know whom to appoint to the position. They asked the greatest rabbis, but none had a solution. Then they came to Yampol to the "Noda BiYehuda" and he solved the riddle. "Perhaps Rabbi Meir [is right] who disagrees with the talmudic statement that [we assume a dying man is among] the majority of those on their deathbed who do in fact die, and he takes into account the few who survive since there are a few who survive, and therefore there is no need to consider who would replace him since he might survive." This solution pleased them, and they decided to appoint the Gaon the Noda BiYehuda as their rabbi, and sent for him with great honor and admiration. The residents of our city of Yampol requested him to return here, but he was not inclined to follow that course. In his book [Noda BiYehuda] is printed a letter from his son the gaon Rabbi Yaakovka saying that his father was rabbi and Rosh Yeshiva here for a decade. It is also known that the [author of] "Hafla'ah" [Rabbi Pinchas Horowitz of Frankfurt] sent a letter to the Mechutan of the Noda BiYehuda that he should request that the Noda BiYehuda live in peace and friendship with the tzaddik Rabbi Michal, the Maggid of Zloczow, who was then living in Yampol, Volhyn. Besides his handwriting and signature exist since his time in the register of our Chevra Kadisha. This is the absolute truth, do not think otherwise."

Copied from the Ledger itself

With the help of G-d

With Mazal Tov we are affirming the regulations which were made by the members of the rules committee who were chosen in the presence of the entire Chevra Kadisha.

The electors will appoint four officers. Two in place of the two trustees and two in charge of visiting the ill. Now, immediately all the members of the Chevra Kadisha will elect by majority one trustee for a three year term. This trustee will have no other appointment, he will be responsible overall. He will be in charge of all the Chevra Kadisha's expenditures and income. All pledges will be entrusted to him and all expenditures will be through him, all monies will pass through his hands. He is not permitted to release even a single Prutah without a receipt from the monthly officer, and the officer will immediately record the receipt in the ledger. The trustee will hold the receipt until the auditing, and any expenditure without a receipt will not be taken into account. Whenever a pledge is received it will be immediately recorded in the ledger and so also when the pledge is redeemed.

The trustee (for three years) will receive a note with the signature of the treasurer each month. More than that requires the signature of all the officers in the city for [expenditures] up to one Ducat. More than that requires the signature of six officials, and the seventh from monies for visiting the ill. Any discounts which will be made to any preacher or any other discounts, or whatever expenditures are necessary for the needs of the Chevra, the trustee will receive only the note of the treasurer, but all purchases will be received by the trustee. The officer in charge of visiting the ill, will visit the ill in the hospice of the destitute every day. Whatever is needed by the ill, the treasurer will give a note to the trustee who will purchase the needs of the ill. All the needs of the hospice, especially since the appointment of the officer in charge of visiting the ill, and all misfortunes (may there be none) when taking pledges all the officers will sit together and when decisions are made all the officers will sit together.

To receive members to the Chevra from among those who were not members this year before Pesach, permission is granted to accept five men into the Chevra with a majority vote of the appointees, there being sixteen appointees. After the end of this year, the Chevra will not accept more than one member each year upon a majority vote of the entire membership. Four negative votes of eligible voters can withhold the acceptance. This is for six years. After the end of six years after the coming Pesach they can be accepted by a majority vote of the entire membership. The exception is children under three years who can be accepted just by the officers!

When there are arbitrators, then whoever holds any appointment at the time of the arbitration cannot transfer his appointment. However, if he has no appointment at all, or if he wants a new appointment which he did not have at the time of the arbitration, although he may have held previously but presently he holds no appointment, then the two other arbitrators cannot embarrass him altogether, they can just choose three others and he will be among the three. The two arbitrators must choose an officer from among these three!

Whatever the Chevra charges for books must be paid from the Chevra's money before any other expenditures which the trustee releases based on notes as above. If he holds no money belonging to the Chevra, then any expenses he incurs will be based on a 'hetter iska' (contract to invest money and circumvent usury prohibitions). Every quarteryear the officers must meet and audit with the trustee all expenses and income which passed through his hands and immediately record it in the ledger. All this in the presence of the rabbi and recorded by the rabbi. All this only as long as the rabbi is here.

From now on, whoever is required to donate a dinner will not be able to redeem it. He must actually give a dinner.

For the Shmini Atzeres dinner, the monthly officer will purchase through the trustee ten pots of honey and the wax will be sold by the trustee and will be for the other needs of the dinner. But he will not spend even one prutah more than that on the needs of the dinner the members of the Chevra will now draw lots and each one in his turn will accompany the officer spend the night with those on their deathbeds or for other duties. Similarly, he will attend Tahara together with the officer and will attend to the ill to provide them with all their needs and all will be given with the approval of the officer and will be recorded in the ledger. The officers are obliged to fulfill all these regulations and all will be done for the sake of Heaven. May it be His will that death be swallowed up eternally, and we will go up joyfully to Jerusalem

Twelve days in the month of Adar in the year 5506

signed Yechezkel Segal Landau

Today, Monday, the tenth of Iyar 5507 all the members of the Chevra in our community gathered together, and those who did not have time to come themselves sent their opinion with their relatives, and they voted and accepted with mazal Reb Zelig son of Reb M. as trustee for three years in accordance with the regulations on the other side of the page by a majority vote. In fact he had two majorities, i.e. a majority of all the members of the Chevra whether related to him or not, and when we discounted all the invalid votes he was chosen in the presence of all the members of the Chevra and will conduct himself exactly in accordance with the regulations on the other side of the page. May G-d give length of days and years to all of Israel held previously but presently he holds no appointment, then the two other arbitrators cannot embarrass him altogether, they can just choose three others and he will be among the three. The two arbitrators must choose an officer from among these three!

Whatever the Chevra charges for books must be paid from the Chevra's money before any other expenditures which the trustee releases based on notes as above. If he holds no money belonging to the Chevra, then any expenses he incurs will be based on a 'hetter iska' (contract to invest money and circumvent usury prohibitions). Every quarteryear the officers must meet and audit with the trustee all expenses and income which passed through his hands and immediately record it in the ledger. All this in the presence of the rabbi and recorded by the rabbi. All this only as long as the rabbi is here.

From now on, whoever is required to donate a dinner will not be able to redeem it. He must actually give a dinner.

For the Shmini Atzeres dinner, the monthly officer will purchase through the trustee ten pots of honey and the wax will be sold by the trustee and will be for the other needs of the dinner. But he will not spend even one prutah more than that on the needs of the dinner the members of the Chevra will now draw lots and each one in his turn will accompany the officer spend the night with those on their deathbeds or for other duties. Similarly, he will attend Tahara together with the officer and will attend to the ill to provide them with all their needs and all will be given with the approval of the officer and will be recorded in the ledger. The officers are obliged to fulfill all these regulations and all will be done for the sake of Heaven. May it be His will that death be swallowed up eternally, and we will go up joyfully to Jerusalem

Twelve days in the month of Adar in the year 5506

signed Yechezkel Segal Landau

Today, Monday, the tenth of Iyar 5507 all the members of the Chevra in our community gathered together, and those who did not have time to come themselves sent their opinion with their relatives, and they voted and accepted with mazal Reb Zelig son of Reb M. as trustee for three years in accordance with the regulations on the other side of the page by a majority vote. In fact he had two majorities, i.e. a majority of all the members of the Chevra whether related to him or not, and when we discounted all the invalid votes he was chosen in the presence of all the members of the Chevra and will conduct himself exactly in accordance with the regulations on the other side of the page. May G-d give length of days and years to all of Israel and may death be swallowed up forever. That which was before me in my home I have written and signed for a record on the above date.

Yechezkel Segal Landau

Today, the second of Tevet 5508 was an auditing with the leader, the respectable Reb Zelig, trustee of the Chevra Kadisha according to notes and [we concluded that the Chevra] owes that leader the amount of two hundred and forty four ducats based on a 'hetter iska' as was audited before me on the above date.

signed Yehezkel Segal Landau

The amendment cited on the other side of the page, that whoever is required to donate a dinner cannot redeem it, is a proper and correct amendment, being that because of this the dinner is delayed after Atseres[*2] until it is forgotten and is never payed at all. However, presently, since the expenses of the Chevra have risen this year because they were involved in the Mitzva of building the courtyard in front of the synagogue, they fell into debts because of high interest. Therefore all the members of the Chevra Kadisha present here have agreed unanimously that why should we eat [a festive dinner at the time we are accruing] interest, and all agreed that each should redeem his dinner with money and the money will be delivered to the rabbi to pay the debts of the Chevra Kadisha so that they do not fall into [debts] for increasingly high rates of interest. Today the fourth day of Sivan 5508.

Yechezkel Segal Landau

Reb Isaac Katz was obliged to give a dinner on all kinds (?) and paid his undertaking (? abbreviation), therefore he is released from his dinner. Reb Yehoshua paid a gold ducat for the dinner he was oblige to give, therefore he is released from providing a dinner. The learned Reb Nachman Charash paid a gold ducat for a large dinner therefore he is released from his obligation to provide a dinner. The learned

Heshel Bathath [abbreviation, probably incorrectly transcribed] paid a gold ducat for a large dinner and is thus released from that dinner. These three ducats, i.e. from Reb Yehoshua and Reb Nachman and Reb Heshel were received by the treasurer Reb Shimon for honey for the dinner of Simchas Torah.

Yechezkel Segal Landau

Today, Monday the fourth of Kislev 5509, in the presence of the entire Chevra, were renewed [the regulation] that all pledges and expenses and income must be through the principal trustee, Reb Zelig, and it is forbidden for any officer to accept any pledge or income, even a single prutah. Just the trustee will pay all the expenditures of the Chevra according to notes on 'hetter hiska' and no note from the officers will be returned unpaid. Also for the coming Simchas Torah the trustee is obliged to purchase six pots of raw honey [to be delivered] to the monthly officer for the purpose of the dinner and the wax will be for the officer for the purpose of the other expenses of the dinner. Other than that he will spend nothing on the dinner. From today on the officers and the trustee will act according to this regulation, and whichever of them acts otherwise will lose. If the officer acts otherwise and accepts any pledge or income then he will lose his appointment. If the trustee returns any note unpaid then no pledge or income may come through him. Also the debt to the trustee on the basis of 'hetter iska' must be paid in the best manner, and all the comunity property [literally 'holy vessels'] are in lien to the trustee. Together with what has been clarified, that the trustee is obliged to pay all the expenses of the Chevra from his own money on the basis of 'hetter iska,' it is stated explicitly that at least four hundred gold ducats will be paid to him [? abbreviation] on the basis of 'hetter iska.' When the trustee is not home then he must appoint another in his place to pay the expenses of the Chevra in a manner that no note will be returned unpaid. All this was decided by a quorum on the abovementioned date. The Sefer Torah of the Chevra which was written by the scribe Nosson Za"l was sold to Reb Yehuda son of Reb Donno Za"l until the twenty sixth of Nissan 5511.

Yechezkel Segal Landau

Today it was agreed by the officers with a cherem that from today on the Shmini Atzeres dinner will be no more than three Kar'b (abbreviation) and there will be no more profits from it, just the treasurer will wait without profit. First whatever the Chevra owes will be paid, whatever was given on profit [I think this means on the basis of the 'hetter iska.'] After that is paid, then the treasurer will be paid for the dinner with the best payment that the Chevra has. It is understood that he will not pay any expenditures except for the purpose of the burial of the destitute, heaven forbid. The Shemini Atzeres dinner is without distributing honey cake and drinking beer. I also affirm all these good [regulations] today Wednesday the twenty sixth of Nissan 5511

Yechezkel Segal Landau

The cherem [ban] has been anulled with regards to this matter. It is permissable to give to the poor and to visiting preachers and other travelers and to any passerby who stretches forth a hand. Also, it is permissable for the Chevra to donate to the repair of the synagogue and other Mitzvot and also to the repair of the cemetery.

Wednesday, the fifth of Tammuz 5513

Yechezkel Segal Landau

GREAT EVENTS IN A SMALL TOWN

[101]

First Jewish inhabitants (in Yampol) came from Gaul, Spain

The famous Gaon (wise man) Reb Yechezkel Landau was one of the town's first rabbis (during the period 1745-1749.) The town becomes a great center for Torah study

The Yampol Bet ha-Midrash (house of study) has closets filled with prayer books and contemporary interpretations of the Torah.

The Righteous Reb Michal Zloczower, student of the Ba'al Shem Tov, became the town's spokesperson

His son Reb Yossel Yampol sits at the head of the dynasty of rabbis

Both father and son are buried in a tomb in the old cemetery

Blood Libel in Yampol (1750-1751.) Storm throughout the Jewish World

Influential Jewish Landlords imprisoned

Rabbi Elyakim, the famous wise man of Yampol was sent as the representative of the Committee of the Four Lands (Poland, Russia, Lithuania and Galicia) to visit the Holy Pope in Rome

After six years of (outside) intervention, the shtetl of Yampol was liberated

Talmudic writer and thinker Reb Yitzchak Ber Levinson (RIBA'L) resides in Yampol for a few years before settling in Kremenetz

The first modern Hebrew teacher Reb Yitchak Goldberg (Itsi Moshe Hersh) and Reb Alter Rimel (Alter Abraham Alikum's) disseminate the teaching of Hebrew in Hebrew, first in the town of Berdichev and second in Ostra

The Jewish youth publish a Hebrew journal in typed form under the name "HaChaya." Only two issues appeared

Hebrew and Yiddish libraries are established in the surrounding towns.

———————

HOLOCAUST SONGS
by Hadassah Rubin

[103]

(A)
A REGARD

Tell me, tell me, you can see, I am not crying.
My eye is empty, the heart turned to stone,
Tell me ...
I want, I want in your words
To find yesteryear once again the gardens
Of yesteryears.
A fence, a hut ... interrupt me -
Today, repeatedly, the place is filled with graves
And from the Valley.
The sky is departing. Interrupt me -
There remained my first joy,
Never to come back.
Tell me, tell me, you can see I am not crying
In black holes in the ground, bones are resting
Not covered with soil.
And from the valley, and from the bones
There is no path leading to anyone
As if the town was dead.
Tell me, tell me, through your words
I find my way to places from the past
Walking with a wobbly step.
I reach the place, the place from where
There is no return
Where the road comes to an end.
Tell me, tell me, you can see, I am not crying
Tell me which of these bones
In the valley asked about me?
Is it possible ... that they have a grudge against me
Because I remained alive?
I, one of the town's inhabitants?
Tell me, tell me, you can see, I am not crying
Like a tomb - my heart turned to stone,
Fenced in with barbed wire!

(B)
MY JEWISH CHILD

The light from the boundless horizon
The total joy
From the wind's breeze
On the silk edge of the grass
From the play of rays
My tender feeling
Without a blemish, without a sin -
For you, my child
For you, the Jewish child.
So in your eyes
Let the reflection shine
In a joyful color.
However, have you understood
Your mother's last outcry
And is it crying out in you?
My hands become empty
Like the void of the desert.
The light is of no use to me any more.
I should have your pain and suffering
My child, my Jewish child.

(C)
COMPASSION

During hot evening
On muggy evenings
I tell myself: have compassion
I tell myself: have compassion
I pat my hands
And I ask of them compassion
Don't rip the body
In bloody thoughts!
In muggy evenings,
With the eyes closed
I look for your, I call you.
My oppressed ones.
In muggy evenings
Don't tell me about compassion
I am the pain
I am the complaint.

OUR SHTETL IS BURNING
by M. Gvirtig

[106]

(A)

It's burning, brothers, it's burning!
Our poor shtetl, pathetically, is burning!
Furious winds with fury
Rip apart, burn and by blowing
Intensify the unrestrained flames
Everything in sight is ablaze!
It's burning, brothers, it's burning!
Out poor shtetl, pitifully, is burning!
The tongues of fire
Have already encircled the entire shtetl
And the furious winds are blowing,
Everything in sight is afire!
It's burning, brothers, it's burning!
It's possible that the moment may come
When the entire shtetl with you in it
Will remain in fire and flames
Like after a fire
Two black empty walls.
It's burning, brothers, it's burning!
The help depends primarily on you
If the shtetl is dear to you
Take the equipment, put out the fire
Put it out with your own blood
Show that you can do it!
Don't stand around, brothers, wasting time looking
With folded hands
Don't stand around, brothers, put out the fire.
Our shtetl is burning!.....

(B)
A DAY OF REVENGE

And I tell you, brothers, remember what I say
The only consolation and compassion:
It will come, you hear! A day will come
Which will avenge us!
Revenge for our suffering and pain -
For the blood which was spilled by our enemies
Revenge for those whose remains
No human being will every find out about ...
Revenge for the deeds which were not even heard of in Sodom
For mothers, orphans, widows

Revenge will cry out from the depth of the earth,
The blood of millions of human sacrifices.
The man will await, but without a doubt, will not see the outcome of
0the war
When our prophet will echo the words:
Revenge! I will take revenge!
The day will come, yes, I hope and believe
I see, brothers, his arrival from afar
And he will bring us joy like a pigeon
A message about the time of freedom.

CHAPTERS FROM YAMPOL MEMOIRS
by David Rubin

[108]

Enlightment and decline in the shtetl - Hassidic rabbis and thousands of Chassidim coming to the Memorial day - Yampol tanners, companies and organizations - Yampol students and synagogue members - The beginning of the Haskalah (Intellectual) period - Establishment of the library - A few resentful people want to close it - We gather our own money for Tzedaka issues - The Zionist movement - The bath-house - Yampol water carriers -Yampol has its own orchestra - The dreadful Cholera epidemic - A wedding in the cemetery.

Chapter 1
A SHTETL FULL OF FAMOUS CHASSIDIM

Among the small towns surrounding Kremenetz (Volhyn region) was also included the town where I was born - Yampol. The Jews from the past, the 18th century, interpreted the origin of the town's name in the following manner: because the town is like an islet surrounded by the river 'Goryn,' it is called 'Yam-Pele' (Hebrew for wonder sea) and the origin of the name goes back to the time of the six days of creation ... from the time when the first man gave every creation, every human being, every language, all towns and villages, as well as the seas and rivers, an appropriate name. There is no doubt as to the fact that the first man was a Jew who spoke only Hebrew, the Holy language ... for this reason, the Jew is the decision maker ...as a result all the Christians who could not speak the Holy language had to break their tongue and say 'Yam-Pol' to this very day ...

Until the end of the 18th century, Yampol was distinguished from the neighboring shtetl by the tombs of 'rabbis' which could be found in the Yampol cemetery. Among the tombstones was a 'tomb' where two righteous Jews were buried ... Reb Michal Zlotsever and his son Reb Yosel Yampoller. Both were buried in a tomb in the old cemetery, located almost within the town's limits.

In the second tomb, in the new cemetery, located a distance from the town, was buried the righteous Reb Yakov-Yosef from Ostra, the grandson of the famous righteous Rabbi Yi'vi, a student of the Ba'al Shem Tov, who resided in Ostra, the author of the famous Chassidic book "Rabbi Yi'vi".

The 26th of the month of Tammuz is the Yarzheit of the death of the Ostra righteous man. On that day Ostra Chassidim came from all corners of the region, wealthy Jews in buggies, merchants in simple wagons drawn by horses, and the poor people on foot. I also believe that Ester Harinshtein, a magnate from Kiev, came to the memorial.

She was from the Brotski family, a devoted Ostra Chassida (she quoted the Rebbe's Torah [insights.]) The grandchildren of the Ostra righteous man, Reb Yosele Kiniver and Reb Alter'uni from Ostra, also came to the 'ceremony.' ...

The grandchildren were of different opinions about the rabbinic dynasty ... both of them wanted to be the 'appointed heir,' 'the bearer of the throne.' The followers of the old rabbi were divided as to who should lead them, a part was behind the 'Kiniver' and a part for 'Ostra' ... this was the reason for their disagreement. Both of the rabbis did everything possible to increase their support. The 'Kiniver' rabbi used to "prepare tables with food," on the other hand, the 'Ostra' rabbi, Rabbi Alter'uni - a great Torah scholar with a sharp mind - served G-d... "with food and drink." With "food and drink" vodka and other liquors were drunk and a variety of food was eaten when he prepared a special table for a special occasion, or even every day when Chassidim came to visit him.

On this above mentioned memorial day, the 'good Jews' (as the Rabbis were referred to) made good business because it is a known fact that every Jew misses something, every Jew has a worry, everyone has a serious problem: one's son is called to the army, someone else's child passes away at an early age, before the child reaches the age of one year it passes away, yet another has to decide about a match for his daughter. If we were to put down every problem, there would not be enough paper on which to write it.

The above mentioned needy people used to pay the rabbi's sexton for writing a note with the following text: Ploni and Ploni, or Plonit and Plonit (Mr. & Mrs.) are in need of a male child, or to make a better living, and asked the rabbi to use his influence on the heaven's government for them to have a male child, alive and well. To the note they added "pidyion"[*3] rich people used to give a lot more. Such notes [in Yiddish: Kvitl] were given to the rabbi by the hundreds with all kinds of requests on them.

The rabbi was held over for Shabbath and with great fanfare was led to pray in the Ostra or Trisker Synagogue After prayer, he sat at the table and read the Torah and other interpretations.

The rabbi's livelihood necessary to maintain his 'household' came from a mandatory monthly payment made by every Chassid. The payment was called 'Ma'amaid.' The rabbi had his sextons travel from town to town collecting the 'Ma'amaid.'

The rabbi also used to visit towns and villages and stay over for Shabbath. He presided over the festivity, read the Torah, took payments, drank and sang ...

Besides the above mentioned 'Kiniver' and 'Ostra' righteous, we were also visited by other grandchildren of righteous men, who brought with them letters of important relationships.

From time to time, we were also visited by the famous "Rachmestrivke" rabbi, Rabbi Dudl (deceased.) Other good Jews also came to visit us, among them the Bazilier Rabbi, Rabbi Yosel David (deceased.) Later on he resided in Proskurow. At the end he was killed by Petlura's [*4] murderers . The Bazilier Rabbi was the rabbi of the craft-shop owners. He was very influential with them.

The town was inhabited by about eight to nine hundred souls, about a hundred and fifty of whom were salaried tailors, shoemakers, carpenters, furriers, blacksmiths, boiler makers, painters, water-carriers and barbers. Of the aforementioned craftsmen some of them made a decent living such as tailors who worked for the noblemen and the tailors who prepared seasonal clothes for the peasants. These tailors employed poor boys and girls who worked for almost no pay. The tailors used to travel from market place to market place.

Chapter 2
YAMPOL'S SHOPKEEPERS

For some time the Yampol shopkeepers were not permitted to open their shops in their homes. All stores had to be located together in the center of town.

The physical layout of the shops was as follows: two long buildings facing each other and joined by two doors. Each building consisted of about thirty rooms. The rooms were separated by wooden planks. Through the cracks in the planks, the shopkeepers could easily observe what was going on in the neighbor's shop ... how much merchandise the neighboring shopkeeper had and evaluate its worth. Each shop had a door which had a square folding platform. The platform opened into a hanging table. The tables were very convenient. The shopkeepers put on them all kinds of items for sale. The doors with the hanging tables were facing each other so the shopkeeper could see what the other shopkeepers were selling ... this was the cause of quarrels, one shopkeeper accusing the other of stealing away the customers with 'winks of the eye' ... at the end of the day, or market fair when the shops were closed. Throughout the night the guard used to bang on the iron barrel to assure everyone that he was not asleep while guarding.

They used to say about the Yampol shopkeepers: "they earn a living but don't have enough money to buy merchandise." Whatever profit they made on selling merchandise they spent on living ... for this reason the shelves were empty of merchandise. Some experienced shopkeepers used to go bankrupt. A wholesaler with many years of experience used to come and make a deal, meaning he received (in payment) only twenty per cent of the value of the entire stock owed ... and once again the credit account was opened and the shopkeeper was in business again.

This happened most of the time with the fabric stores. Other shopkeepers used to pay interest, mortgage their homes and work very hard at making a living. It was terrible when the New Year came and one had to buy out the promissory notes. It was a real tragedy ... because who had money to buy out the promissory note? Solution - people made deals. People who were supposed to buy out the second promissory note were buying the third and the ones who had to purchase the third were buying the fourth or bought nothing at all. The main office used to send their senior employee for an inspection ... when the shopkeepers found out about the inspection (through an unofficial note from the main office) they hid their merchandise during the night so the shops remained with bare, empty shelves ... and the men from the shops went to the synagogue to pray in hope that everything would go well ... only the women remained in the shops, wrapped in old shawls with their faces red and blue from irritation.

The main market fair days in Yampol were on Sunday and every two weeks on Tuesday. On Tuesday, on the market day, buyers and sellers from the surrounding town and cities came to trade The merchants traded a variety of merchandise. Every merchant sold the type of items in which he was a specialist.

This is the way the merchants traded in an attempt to make a living.

Chapter 3
YAMPOL CHEDERS

Yampol had no schools nor classes for that matter. What existed were Cheders (Sunday schools, attended by Jewish children six days a week) where Bible and Rashi and Tanach were taught.

From the health point of view, all Cheders in Yampol were on the lowest level. In a room of about two or three meters, ten to twelve students learned with the rabbi. In the same room, two of the rabbi's daughters, sitting near the bed, were working on a fisherman's net from a large roll of fishing line attached to the bed. They obtained the fishing line from a merchant for whom they were working. The daughters and the craftsmen made ten kopeks each per day. So by Passover they gathered a few rubles, enough to buy for themselves a dress and a pair of shoes ... something which their father could not accomplish from teaching students.

The preschool Cheders looked even worse. About eighteen to twenty students sat in a damp, dark room, with the ceiling reaching almost the top of the table ... the rabbi with the small Tallit, an oily kippah on his head, with a small whip along his side, provided the children with prayer and the fundamentals of the Torah.

The Torah and Rashi Cheders did not look any better than the preschool ones and the students were not any different either. The only difference was in the fact that the rabbi's daughters were not knitting a fisherman's net but were plucking chicken feathers for the mothers of the students, making the same money as the other two daughters and working toward the same goal.

Chapter 4
YAMPOL BET MIDRASHIM

Among the Yampol homes which reached about 150 in number, there stood like a giant among midgets, the Yampol Synagogue. The interior of the synagogue looked as follows: the dome of the synagogue was artistically decorated with the twelve signs of the Zodiac ... two thick white columns supported the upper part of the building, the Holy Ark, rows of painted and polished benches and stands. The interior of the synagogue was very nicely arranged. The Yampol synagogue was in no way inferior to the surrounding synagogues in the largest towns nearby.

At the time, the entrance and the reflecting lights were also not inferior ... a narrow street separated the synagogue from the Beit Midrash and from the Trisker home of prayer. Nearby, across the street, was an Ostra home of prayer. The synagogue followed the 'Ashkenazi' way of praying, the remaining home of prayer the 'Sephardic' way.

Most of the people who prayed in the synagogue were proprietors of craft workshops, there were few aristocrats such as the paramedic, the lawyer, the representative of the 'Singer sewing machines' ... smoking and drinking of liquor at a memorial service were always forbidden. The leadership and sextons in the synagogue came from the working class of people.

The majority, including butchers, shopkeepers, people working in the village, small merchants, all prayed in the Beit Midrash. In the Beit Midrash, people smoked cigarettes, drank liquor, learned Mishnayes and Shulchan Aruch. Every day three to four minyan sessions were held in the Beit Midrash, while in the synagogue there was only one in the morning and one in the evening. Often the Beit Midrash was visited by poor people from afar who stayed overnight. Homeowners used to provide them with shelter. The Beit Midrash was often visited by booksellers. They used to spread their books with large print on the table: Tchinot for lighting candles, for memorial services, for blowing the shofar ... for children interesting novels and other important books. The majority of the town's people prayed in the Beit Midrash. It is a well known fact that every Jew wishes to be called to the Torah reading. Obviously it was impossible to call everyone to read the Torah so on Shabbath and the Holidays it was necessary to 'call' people to the Torah at a table, away from the bimah .. While the rich, the important homeowners were called to the Torah on the bimah, the majority the simple, poor folk, were given Torah calls at the table away from the bimah.

In the Trisker prayer home prayed Trisker, Zinkever, Ralhastrivker, and Makarever Chassidim. Here, people were deeply involved in the study of the Torah, with great devotion. Also elderly people sat in deep thought in contemplation of a difficult to understand passage or some other interesting passage.

The above mentioned Trisker prayer home was different from all other ones in Yampol because the 'Vitsmah Furnkah'[*5] was added to the Kaddish prayer in the Trisker home. In the Ostra prayer home it was forbidden to say the 'Vitsmah Furnkah.' For this reason the Hassidim were ready to break bones ... in the same prayer home one could not come in wearing a straw hat.[*6] Many people were verbally abused for doing it.

In the Ostra prayer home as in the Trisker prayer home, young men and older ones, after Bar Mitzvah until they were married, as well as those who were already married and supported by their fathers-in-law, sat in the prayer rooms and learned the Torah studying to become rabbis, cantors, religious slaughterers, etc.

Chapter 5
BEGINNING OF THE INTELLECTUAL MOVEMENT

Aforementioned Yampol Cheder teachers taught their students only Torah. However at the end of the eighteenth century, the first signs of a new period were brought to town. An educated man, the son-in-law of Dayan Alter r' David's, as he was called, came to Yampol. He taught the children grammar according to the book. He and another educated man, Yaakov Railes, obtained secular books from somewhere and began to read them secretly. They also gave the books to others if asked for them. Alter r' David's did not play an important role in spreading intellectual thought among the youth of Yampol because he had only a few students. The Yampol fathers looked upon Alter as an unbeliever ... they did not want him to teach their children and "change them into Christians" ... and without a doubt they had evidence about it ... first, Alter wore a high paper collar with two points bent downwards; second, he wore a penguin coat with a split in the back; third, he actually shook girls' hands; fourth, it was said that he gives his beard a rest ... he shortens it, if not with scissors, he pulls or bites on it with his teeth; fifth, he smelled of something - they believe it was 'perfume'. As for smoking cigarettes on Shabbath there were 'those who said he did. A neighbor of Alter's noticed in his room, on Shabbath, after the kugl, a burnt out match. He asked: "Is it possible that Alter's wife did not clean the room for Shabbath, and sweep the dust from the floor?" How did it come about? I remember as if it were yesterday. I was his student. Alter r' David's was a capable man, a well rounded person ... a good engraver, a good mathematician. He also had a good musical ear, sang nicely and had a good voice with a lot of feeling. It once happened that the Shul public prayer man leading the prayer on Yom Kippur became sick and did not show up for afternoon prayer. The synagogue was searching for a replacement to lead the early evening prayer. Some of the younger people mentioned the name of Alter r' David's, that he should lead the prayer. However, the majority was against this suggestion ... the only reason for rejection was the fact that he was an epikoros! This is how the umbilical cord of intellectual life in Yampol took roots.

Chapter 6
YAMPOL SOCIETY

The Yampol Jews were divided into societies: 'society of caring for the sick,' 'burial society,' 'society for the needy,' 'society of the praying man.' The management of the society for the caring of the sick and the burial society was in the hands of two of the town's rich men. They did not let go of the reins of controlling the societies for two reasons: firstly, the societies brought in income because when someone passed away the first thing which had to be done was to pay for the burial place ... and there was no actual price for the burial place. One asked for the place as much as it was possible to get for it. Once one received a permit from the sexton of the synagogue allowing the burial of the deceased, then one contacted the burial carriers ... another source of a few rubles ... for this reason it was important to control these two organizations To confuse the thought of the electorate of the community, the aforementioned controllers, on Simchat Torah, organized a party where cake, liquor and honey was consumed - as much as one's heart desired for whoever wanted it. Once everybody had their fill they obviously went to elect the same rich men ...

The other societies barely made out ... every member had to contribute a few kopeks which were supposed to pay for the administrative expense. They also had a Kiddush ... which was taken from weekly contributions. The free loan society with the ten rubles of mandatory contribution from each member could help the most needy with a free loan to be repaid in installations. The loan was three times the membership fee i.e. thirty rubles. So the most one had to wait was until the money could be returned so a new loan could be taken out.

The Jewish Mayor in Yampol was in the hands of the town's rich men and all efforts were made to make sure that the Mayor was 'their man.'

The rabbi was hired with the agreement of the rich men.

Chapter 7
YAMPOL'S BATHHOUSES

Believe it or not, Yampol did have a bathhouse and it looked as follows: by a stream (a small tributary of the wide Horin river) stood an old building. In the building, Dina the bathhouse lady sat ... next to her lay "brushes made from oak" and everyone who barely made it to Friday gladly paid two kopeks for the brushes and walked into the second room ... there on a cement floor sat naked Jews, with red bodies, breathing heavily. They just came out of the fire. From there the men ran through a corridor where on the right side were two large burning ovens, heating the walls of the bathhouse and the kettle full of water.

Twenty meters from the bathhouse, parallel to it, was the holy bathhouse. Outside, painted white, with two glass windows, inside a small home - on the right side a large room with six wooden beds, on the left a kitchen where the windows were boarded up.

A few sick people rested in the room. The sick were visited twice a week by a paramedic. The same arrangement was true for supplying food to the sick. This held true for many years, the same bathhouse, the same mikvah, the same sick house.

Chapter 8
THE SEXTON WAKES UP THE JEWS

In some of the towns surrounding Yampol, there was a tradition whereby every night, after midnight, after 2 a.m., the sexton used to walk the streets and woke up the Jews with a sad singing voice: "Israel, the holy people, wake up to work" and similar phrases which matched the first phrase ... Yampol's sexton did not sing. Instead he used a wooden hammer to knock three times at the wooden window blinds of the homes. The first two knocks followed each other while the third one was after a pause ... this event took place after every midnight. When it happened that someone in the town was "missing" (passed away) ... in many homes the memorial candle was lit, and the man of the house washed his nails ... then he went out into the street and listened to the two knocks which the sexton continued to make in the adjacent street. And when a door from a nearby house was opened with a screech, a question pierced the night: "who passed away?"

Chapter 9
YAMPOL SYNAGOGUE GOERS

Young men and small children did not need the sexton to knock on the door ... by habit, by inertia, they woke up after midnight and from time to time even before midnight, to go to the synagogue where they sang: "Oy, oy, oy, said our father! Oy, oy, oy, said the rabbi!" and with heartrending envy every one of the 'students' listened to the high pitched voices of their friend who brought to the light of the world the sweet melody.

The 'synagogue people' (people who studied in the synagogue) divided themselves into groups. The first group were the sons-in-law, the children of the rich father-in-law and mother-in-law. Their father bought them from purity, meaning that besides the dowry which was deposited with the town's rich man at two per cent interest a year, the father of the bride, now their father-in-law (the marriages were arranged at a very early age), was committed to fully support the son-in-law in the best of style for a good few years. On the other hand, the son-in-law was obligated to study until such time as he could get Smicha from the Alt-Kastantiner rabbi, or become a wise student of the Bible.

The second group were the young men who sat in the synagogue for a few years who were presented as a 'precious stone' to be caught by a young lady. The third group were students who just completed the Cheder, some of whom came because their father could not pay any more for the studies in the Cheder. They came to the synagogue to develop intellectually on their own.

Truly, the synagogue produced wise students and teachers, especially in the Talmud, Midrash and P'sukim. Besides the previously mentioned intellectuals, Alter r' David's and Yaacov Railes, there were two older synagogue people who are worth mentioning here. They were the first 'breakers of the fence' who pushed the youth in the direction of the light (intellectual freedom), secular knowledge. One was named Hershel from Moier (Garbarz), the second was Mosher Alter Student (Grynshpan). In addition to learning the Gemarra, they also studied other books. They learned math and algebra. They played an important role in our development. Hershel from Moier was murdered by the Nazis.* The synagogue people Hershel and Moshe were in hiding in the orchard. One was killed and the other wounded. Moshe eventually left to go to America where he is till this very day. Hershel read secular books and had a considerable influence on the young people of Yampol. The influence was so intense that many times the students used to hide secular reading materials between the pages of the interpretation of the bible.

*His influence was very good and positive. Every winter evening he had a custom of coming to the kloiz and studying the book, "Yad Chazakah" of Maimonides, as well as other philosophical works. He encouraged the boys of the kloiz to keep on studying.

Chapter 10
THE INTELLECTUAL PERIOD

In the year 1900, at the age of eighteen, a few youths celebrated the turn of the century. This was also the year we decided to establish a library. Together with a few of my friends, I organized a group responsible for the library. We sent away three rubles for a subscription to "Zargon" and a few other Yiddish books ...

The first few Yiddish books we purchased were the foundation of the future "Hebrew library" and slowly the library began to develop. We gradually attracted readers and they brought in membership fees of five kopeks a week.

Our Hebrew library, as we called it, already had four hundred books, together with the Hebrew books. In our library we had the works David Frishman, selected works, David's memoirs. Jewish Youth from the surrounding towns came to take out books. The youth were also interested in the library's organization.

A few people in town who were envious of us worried about their youths who came over to our camp. They called for a general meeting where they accused us of creating the terrible situation and where this could lead the Jewish youth. With the approval of the people at the meeting it was decided to destroy the library.

Naturally we did not like the decision considering that the library was developed with so much effort ... we had no other choice but to physically oppose the resolution.

However, this did not stop the few fanatics from their fight. It was on a nice day when we were ordered to appear before the local official. We had to go. In the office I met my friend Ezriel Peretz who was as white as the wall (he was also killed by Hitler.) Frightened, we looked at each other awaiting the unknown.

We did not say a word but our hearts were pounding. What could we do? We all thought we were lost!

Surprisingly, a prominent Jew of the community entered the office, one of the progressive ones who was opposed to the fanatics. So when the representative poured out his heart to the prominent Jew, how he had to fight with the Jewish socialists, the Jew asked him to step into another room and gave him a piece of his mind ... and they let us go. However, he confiscated many books which were not even censored. As is known, every action causes a reaction. This happened in our situation. The organizers of the library and its members began to develop the library with newly found courage. At the beginning of the 20th century, the library contained 1,500 books.

Chapter 11
YAMPOL JEWS GIVE CHARITY

I am doubtful whether you know the meaning of "half-big," so let me tell you about it:

A long time ago, a really long time ago, the Russian ruble was changed into a bilan, which was made from brass or copper coins, starting with dyenichkas, groshes, kopeks -- 3 groshe coins and 2-, 3-, or 5-kopek coins. A ruble was exchanged for either 400 dyenichkas or 200 groshes, and also 100 kopeks for silver coins - 10- kopek coins, 20-kopek and 50-kopek coins. Yampol Jews, and possibly Jews in other cities, used to call a groshe in Hebrew a "big one" without noticing that the Hebrew "gadol" means "big." The groshe was [on the contrary] in fact the smallest coin, just like in Hebrew a blind person is called "sagi nahor" which in Yiddish means "a person with enough light." [Apparently there was a pun on the word groshe in relation to "groyse" - big in Yiddish - D.G.]

In general, when we realize that a "big one" means a groshe, it becomes as clear as day that the "half-big" means a half-groshe or a dyenechka which at the end of the 19th century were already out of circulation, and the Russian bilan was made up of groshes.

Now to the point:

Yampol Jews considered giving charity to be a very important thing, and had very straightforward ideas about this: "Eser" [10] was for wealth ["Ashir"]. "Give a ten-coin for an odd job, and you will become rich." Also "charity saves one from death," and "repentance, prayer and charity remove the evil decree" "charity annuls the evil decrees already issued." The Yampol Jews would give a contribution to the poor with a pleasant demeanor and were therefore renowned as large philanthropists. Large groups of poor people used to flood the town and settle down in the synagogue to "sell their wares." Right after the evening service the congregants, the people working for a living, used to "grab" home a guest. The housewife, the Jewish lady, would fill the table with delicacies: a bit of herring with a slice of onion on a cracker, accompanied with very sour vinegar with a couple of potatoes and bread. This was considered a meal made for a king.

In the morning, the poor folk would move out like a swarm of locusts in town. G-d knows the truth, that the largest part of Yampol Jews had no ability to provide contributions for all of the poor. Would anyone have dared to say that he didn't have the means and circumstances to help out? You had to contribute, you had to give!

For Yampol Jews, charity was the first priority. As religious Jews, they were motivated by sayings from the Bible such as: "Give a tenth of your earnings, so you will get rich," "Charity will save you from death," "Repentance, prayer and charity save you from bad decrees."

The above reputation was well known to beggars and collectors who came to Yampol in numbers out of proportion to what might have been expected. Those out-of-towners used to come into the synagogue and after the evening prayers would spread out into all parts of Yampol where they were treated as guests by their hosts, the kind Jews of Yampol. Here, the compassionate housewives showed their kindness by treating their guests with the best food they had such as a piece of herring, some slices of onion dipped in sour vinegar, a few potatoes and bread. In the morning they would again fan out through the town for their collections. No Yampol Jew would ever say "I am unable to give you charity" though, in one day, you might have to face thirty to forty collectors, so it was not easy to keep up with the big charities.

The local currency was the ruble, which was subdivided into 100 kopeks, ending up with one kopek and one half kopek. The privileged collector had to be given 10 or 20 kopeks. In a case of assistance to a bride it meant having to give a larger amount of charity. For the financial conditions of Yampol Jews, charity became a sizeable part of their budget. When the Czar re-evaluated the currency, he eliminated the half kopek. This meant a special hardship for Yampol Jews, whose common alms were no more than half a kopek. An urgent emergency meeting was called at the synagogue trying to find a solution to the current coin change. The rabbi and representatives of the local grocers debated the problem and Reb Pesach Sofer came up with a practical solution. As there was no longer a brass or copper coin valued at half a kopek, he would prepare some small pieces of parchment which had written on them half kopek. These would be used by Yampol charity givers and later redeemed for actual money by the grocery man Pesach Sofer. This was a beneficent action for the giver as well as the taker, despite the fact that it included a small deduction which was given to Reb Pesach Sofer for his work.

Chapter 12
THE ZIONIST MOVEMENT IN YAMPOL

The young generation of Yampol Jew was well aware of the low standard lack of opportunities and the Czar's restrictions for Jewish trade, commerce and the professions. They felt discriminated against and deprived, downtrodden and humiliated, feelings rooted in anti-Semitism in Yampol. The prohibition of land ownership meant an unjustified denial, as well as a common accusation, of the Christian population calling them the 'people of the air.'

It was an embarrassing, degrading term. Some young people wanted to emigrate to Argentina where they became farmers and prided themselves in the use of the motto "In the plough lies the blessing." No wonder the time was so ripe for Herzl's idea of a Jewish state. It acted as a beam of light for the dark, somber mood of the young Yampol Jews. It sounded great: Herzl planned to buy territory in Palestine from the Turks or establish an independent Jewish state in Uganda. What better hope for a brighter tomorrow could one have? The dream of independence was so powerful, it became ingrained in their minds, even if it might turn out to be self-deception. When Herzl's plan did not materialize, Yampol Jews sank into deep depression. Soon afterwards, the Russo-Japanese war broke out, which completely ended the Zionist's hope for an independent state. It is worth noting, however, that Yampol produced some Zionist writers whose ideas eventually penetrated into the USA, Argentina and Palestine.

When the news that Herzl passed away reached Yampol, the people got together in the large synagogue and mourned in great desperation. Fortunately the Hebrew teacher, Alter Rimel, gave an inspiring speech and made participants take it upon themselves to perpetuate the 'Zionist Ideal' and remain loyal to Zionism.

Chapter 13
THE WATER CARRIERS OF YAMPOL

The elders from the last century claim that the monopoly of water carrying belonged to the old Abraham Ber. Not to say that he became wealthy by his profession, but it is a fact that you could make a living from it without the need for capital investment, or having to pay taxes. There is no doubt in anyone's mind that two rivers surrounding Yampol were at Abraham Ber's disposal and he did not need a license to use them in order to provide water for Yampol's Jews. His son, Shabse, was not too excited that he might inherit his father's profession. He was burdened by a large family consisting of his old father, Abraham Ber, his wife, two sons, two daughters and also Elinke (a diminutive of Elie.) The writer does not know if he was the father's brother or another son. Elie served in the Czar's army as a musician and brought home his clarinet. This gave Shabse the idea that he could also become a musician, a much more prestigious profession than a water carrier. The profession of his father slowly crept out of the family's monopoly.

Chapter 14
YAMPOL GETS ITS OWN MUSIC GROUP

Shabse's family had a spark igniting within for him to become a musician. The talent was actually inherited from his father, the old Abraham Ber. In addition to his work as a water-carrier, he owned a drum and was proud to play on it. When Elie came home from the army with a clarinet, it whetted Shabse's appetite to become part of an orchestra, head by Elie. They formed an orchestra consisting of two drummers and one clarinet, which was favorably accepted by the Yampol community. It was certainly cheaper to hire them than to bring an orchestra from another town. They played at weddings and at the time somebody gave a Sefer Torah to a synagogue. When young people made a gathering they were happy to have Elie's orchestra playing for them.

The Shabse family now made a better living than others. Earnings came from water-carrying, fishing and musical performances. Elie was an ambitious and capable man. He made some money by playing in private homes on Purim, getting paid ten to twenty kopeks, sometimes even a whole ruble. It was too good to be true. Only good for as long as it lasted. Unexpectedly, he ran out of luck. A cholera epidemic broke out in the town and all the good things Shabse's family had enjoyed came to an end.

Chapter 15
A WEDDING AT THE CEMETERY

"You will certainly ask 'what the connection is between a wedding canopy (chuppah) over a cemetery and the Yampol water carriers?'"

The cholera epidemic was very severe. There were casualties in every house. The sanitary committee's recommendations were to smear the walls of every house with whitewash and to pour carbolic acid on the garbage, to boil their water and to have young children recite special prayers. It was all to no avail. A special meeting was called and the following decision was made: "The town would arrange for the marriage of a poor spinster, the ceremony to take place at the local cemetery." This would be the remedy to stop the epidemic. They found the proper 'old maid' in Yampol. The town's 'son-in-law' was located and imported from Wishegrod. The conditions were that the town's Jews had to provide him with a place to live and an occupation by which he could make a living. The occupation to be provided - water carrier thereby becoming severe competition for the Shabse family! A second 'competitor' for Pinchas, the new husband, was Berel, the water-carrier. Some people who lived close to the river were of the idea that they could provide themselves with pails of water, without having to have it delivered.

Elie was a privileged person - having served in the Czar's army he had a license to open a store of alcoholic beverages or to become a letter carrier. But those permits had no value for Elie. The whole of his family were illiterate. That is they could not write or master basic arithmetic. Elie found out that the public baths needed an attendant, applied for the position and got it. It was a good source of income, at least for the next few years. But an ardent anti-Semite had his eyes on the position. With the help of the local priest, he kept on denouncing Elie, accusing him of violations in the upkeep of the public bath. Many inspections were made without any fault being found. The nationalistic Russian Party spouted propaganda: "Beat up the Jews", "'Take away their stores", "Expel them from the village" etc. Thus Jewish life became precarious, completely unprotected by the government. At that time there befell a great tragedy on the Shabse family. Antashke Roshkolnik very much wanted Elie's position. So much so that he came to the public bath, asked for a bunch of leaves to be used there and refused to pay for it. An argument ensued and the instigator then threw Elie into the boiling water causing his instant death.

The Abraham Ber 'dynasty' lost its breadwinner and Yampol had an omen of that which might befall them in their lives in the future.

IMAGES OF YAMPOLLER SOCIETY
by Ezriel Goren

[123]

Chapter One

It is difficult to eulogise a friend and a relative but it is much more difficult to eulogise a whole community that has painfully perished. It seems that they were all born here in the four or five parallel streets, all learned Aleph-Bet with the same Menashe Melamed (Menashe the Teacher), and still what a difference there was. Everyone had his own ways, his own feelings his own way of life. I feel that we must, at the least, erect a small monument for the dear little town with its four or five parallel streets, with the nice cold Shul, with the Prayer House, with the old Trisker Study House. We must issue a small memorial book, like the small town where we first saw G-d's world. A person's memory is weak. During his speedily passing life he sees so many places, meets such a large number of people, hears and survives so many events, that in the end he experiences such a mix of dreams and reality that it is very difficult for me to concentrate my thoughts on the true picture of my little town as it truly reflected in my young childhood soul.

The small houses were almost all built in the same style, nobody could see through the windows what was happening at his neighbor's. A high wall without windows separated one house from the other. The streets were aligned like strings on a violin. The houses were crowded, one next to the other, but every home was a private castle. If I want to describe individual types of the now dead and poor little town, I must refer to the prayer houses. My father was a member of the Trisker Synagogue. Childhood and boyhood impressions have remained in my memory, even though a little cloudy, but still deep enough to be able to be refreshed. At the first place among the stands at the East Wall corner of the South side, prayed Rabbi Shimele, a short thin Jew, always immersed in the Holy Book, who did not speak to anyone, was not even diverted for one minute from the prayer book or the reading of the Torah. In my youthful fantasy he used to appear like a disciple of Rov Liebush. In reality there was something similar between the two - a deep spirituality. Also, far from the everyday, there was something of a certain calm which was expressed in their faces.

When I now want to refresh my memory I can say that at the time the Rabbi's eyes were full of worry, even with a bit of pain. Reb Shimele's appearance always remained calm. I could even say a bit childish. Reb Shimele served G-d with great conviction, whatever he did was in G-d's name.

Chapter Two
REB YISROEL FEIVISHES

Reb Yisroel was the Gemorra teacher but it was not only Gemorra that we learned in his Cheder but also Tanach and Rashi. We learned the Sedra for each week. I must truthfully say that the first year was taken up with getting used to the Rebbe's hoarse voice. Reb Yisroel had a very hoarse voice. We, the pupils, got the meaning of his explanations through the sheen of his big black eyes much more quickly than when his voice strolled through his atrophied throat and mouth. We surmised more than we understood. In the course of two or three years that we learned in his Cheder we managed to at least accumulate some ideas in Gemara, Tanach and Yiddishkeit.

At the gentile's New Year, when the study of Torah was forbidden, Reb Yisroel used to pull out the big drawer of the table, searched for and was able to find a yellowed sheet of paper, written on both sides, and read through the biography of "that person."[*7]

His oldest son, Reb Itzi, so went the rumor among the pupils, lost his mind from deep and prolonged study and ended his life tragically. Reb Yisroel had pleasure only from his son Ben-Zion and his daughter Rachel, a girl with two beautiful eyes and a thick braid. On the eve of Passover, when the Rebbe reviewed the Song of Songs with us, many of us looked with longing at Rachel, the Rebbe's daughter, when she ran through the Cheder.

Reb Yisroel also led the worship service from the pulpit. On the Days of Awe, he used to participate in the "King Sat on His Throne" [*8] I will never forget his rapidly rising from the table in the Trisker Synagogue with the traditional chant of the Days of Awe, strolling and singing the whole way until he reached the pulpit. He, himself, could hardly make a living but on the Sabbath or before a Holiday, he used to collect from the more affluent citizens their contributions for all the poor families.

While speaking of the Yampoller teachers, I must add something about Reb Yosel Berishes' Cheder. I attended his Cheder to listen to his singing on Holidays, especially on Simchat Torah. I still sing his Gentile-Chaddisic song: "Marku, Marku, Shah, Ti Robit Na Yarmake Ni Kupiuesh, Ni Turuish, Tilko Rubish." The translation is clear: "Yid, Yid, what do you do and what do you buy at the market place? You do not buy, you do not sell, you only make fights at the market place."

Yosel Berish had a hard life. His wife, Chasie, was a little weak in the head and the children ran off to the big cities but he took the pain with dignity. I must mention another teacher, Reb Zinvill - a quiet, small Jew. unassuming, without much wisdom. He used to sit at a table with his pupils, holding forth, straining his heart, not sparing his strength, His wife, however, a big, heavy woman, a store keeper, pursued everything possible - she ran to the market place and tried to trade. With regard to his daughter, Udel, I do not know what happened to her.

Chapter Three
THE THREE BIGGER HOUSES

At the west side of our town, near Tekhemlye, three nice houses stood out. In one big house lived the aristocratic Jewish family of Reb Michel Yaolam, a rich Jew, dressed in the European fashion. His children studied in the Gymnasium and in the Music Conservatory. He had the first place at the East Wall on the left side of the Sanctuary. We, the cheder boys, went wild when the family Yaolam used to go out with their own horses and coach and their own coachmen. I do not know much about this family. I only recall that the Rebbe Yisroel used to reproach us and show and point out Michel Yaolam's brother used to study music and eventually became a klezmer at weddings in the United States. Michel Yaolam's children left the town and settled in other countries.

The second house belonged to the second rich man, Reb Dovid Kertman, a rich Jew who dressed in the European fashion, had his own horses and coachmen, a big house made of red bricks and a big stable for horses, coachmen and coach. He did business with the wealthy Polish gentry and was friendly with Graf L. In his home the Maskilim [enlightened people] of the town used to gather, played cards quite often and occasionally drank alcoholic beverages. His wife, from a big city, never left the house to go outdoors and disdained the other Jewish women.

The third house belonged to Berish Boruch's (or Berish Kniff's.) About this Trisker Chassid it can be said: "Whoever honors his wife also honors his children, his neighbors, all residents, as well as the people in the nearby towns that he visits." This was a clever, quiet Jew, a Chassid only two or three levels below the Trisker Rabbi. His older children married well. His son, Itzik, studied without a teacher and knew French perfectly. He was also a good violinist His younger brother, Yudl, also played the violin. This was a very respectable and fine family. If I were to make a comparison between the two rich men, Berish Kniff and Dovid Kertman, I must note that Berish Boruch's was embraced by all the inhabitants of the town. He was, as it is said.[fulfilling his obligations] "To G-d and to people."

Chapter Four
REB YISROEL SHOICHET

While talking about Chassidim, I must say something about Reb Yisroel Shoichet. Reb Yisroel Shoichet was a Staliner Chassid, a teacher, a pious man with a good talent for telling various Chassidic tales. Reb Yisroel also possessed a remarkable memory. He remembered all familial events of all the saintly and good men, starting with the Maggid [preacher] and ending with the youngest grandchild of the Staliner Rabbi.

I am reminded how on a holiday evening, a substantial group of Jews used to gather around him and even we boys used to 'lend an ear' to hear his remarkable stories as well as his personal memories about Rabbis, saints and Chassidim. His older son, Reb Leib, from his first wife, would also join in after completing his studies. He learned Tanach with Ibn Ezra.

With his second wife, Fruma, I also remember the daughters, Chaya and Tzirl, who were ardent followers of Shneir and Dinezon's novels. Shneir novels, in those good times when every writer and critic poured angry criticism about Shneir novels, I must and will justify his novels and point out two positive sides of his writings; first, he taught Jewish daughters to read and second, he opened a wide window to the new rich country America, and that way helped the emigration of the small Jewish towns in Poland, Lithuania and the Ukraine. At the end of the 19th century, the economic situation worsened from year to year and those grown Jewish girls began to influence their parents towards emigrating to America. A free, rich and secure life smiled at the avid young readers of Shneir novels. More than a Jubilee year passed by those youthful years when on holidays before evening prayer, a sizeable group of Jews dressed in their black holiday caftans, would surround Reb Yisroel and he with his sweet voice would tell of miracles, legends from the Ruziner Rabbi Yisroel or from the Staliner Rabbi with his royal court. We, a small group, would listen from the side to the beautiful stories until the very end.

Chapter Five
THE OTHER PEOPLE WHO PRAYED

The other people who prayed at the Trisker Synagogue have dried up and vanished from memory in the course of approximately sixty years and many times I stretch my memory and run through the occupants of these benches. East, south, west and north and the middle benches, on both sides of the platform - all occupied by rugged Jews, teachers and others. The picture reflected in my mind and my memory is hazy and overflowing, cloudy and full of despair.

I owe a debt and feel like erecting a small memorial on my father's grave: "Reb Boruch, son of David Garingut," born in a village settled by German colonists not far from Lutsk. He studied Tanach and Talmud with a relative, a well-known teacher, in Baremel. Between the ages of 17 and 18 he married Pearl Yachtzes of Yampol, where he continued his studies. I did not fully understand him but my father's serious tone made a big impression on me, it evoked a spiritual thirst to understand and feel more deeply..

I recall one episode; my father and another of the students, as well a I (a young lad) walked together. The conversation and discussion was about two giants, Reb Eliezer Mitoar and Reb Yehoshua. Reb Eliezer shouts, "The walls of the Prayer House will show who tells the truth." Then Reb Eliezer calls out in a voice from above [akin to prophecy] which confirms Reb Eliezer's opinion. Reb Yehoshua, however, is not fearful and says that some rabbis are against Reb Eliezer's judgement. My father, Reb Boruch, investigated and explained the miracles of Reb Eliezer as a mark of Reb Eliezer's strong belief in the true law according to his own judgement. My father, Reb Boruch, died and is buried in the old Haifa cemetery.

Chapter Six
OTHER YAMPOLLER TYPES

Like a fresh spring wind that blows through G-d's world, here it shakes the trees as if it is whispering some secret to them: "Arise to do the Creator's work. Enough of shaking and fearing the raging winds and the cold snowy clouds." Spring has come, the wind is still blowing and whispering a message to the sleeping peasant that it is time to harness the oxen, get out to the open field, plow the cold soil and hide the beautiful golden seeds in its lap. The refreshing wind, however, has its own laws. It does not blow wild and raging. It passes through quietly and calmly and only the tops of the taller branches, those who dared and stretched out to the sun in order to catch a ray of sun to see the world of light, those were the spiritually rich Jewish youth. This awakened Jewish youth from whom later developed the stormy thirst for cultural and national aspirations.

I catch a neighbor and ask a question: "How is it, for example, that Reb Doody Dayan got up and left for Israel at age 70 and set up a homestead and even bought a little house in the north?" How did it come to Reb Alter, a Maskil [intellectual] who always dressed well, with a big shiny forehead, who was into deep speculative thinking but also had golden hands for various delicate metal and wood work? I was told that in his last hours, he screamed from fever: "I need tools and instruments for my work." He used to complain to me that his memory had weakened and insisted that he must review the Tanach and Rashi as this would remind him of his younger years and it might strengthen his memory.

How did young people appear, as for example Edel Becker, who used to come to the Synagogue on Saturday, put on his prayer shawl, and read through the Sedra of the week using his new pointer, and Motel Gasses who found it his responsibility to lead us to philosophy and ethics?

That is how Yampoller types were.

YAMPOLLER HOLY MEN
by Hershel Zuckerman

[129]

With G-d's help. Rosh Chodesh Sivan 5722 [1962], Chicago

Dear Mr. A.L. Gellman, Shalom!

Dear Friend, I received your letter while I was in the hospital. I first returned home last week, even now I lie in bed more than I walk and I find writing a little difficult. I am certainly in agreement with the idea of memorializing the memory of the Yampoller Holy Men, but regretfully I do not know how much I can contribute. I did not even know my own father well enough, which means that I simply did not have the power of observation to study his personality. Though two things, which are almost the same, made a special impression on me when I was quite young. They happened when we still lived in the house that belonged to Litman.

On Friday evening, just before nightfall, a telegram came from Ludmir saying that his 36 year old daughter had died. He removed his shoes and sat Shivah for a short while. He then put on his shoes and left for the Synagogue to pray. For the whole Sabbath 24-hour observance he did not show any sign of mourning. Only after Havdalah did he break out in heart-rending sobs.

Something similar occurred a few years later when a boy of eighteen died on Friday night. Early on Saturday morning, his sister Teme, who lived by Natan Melamed, came to the house sobbing. He did not let her into the house saying that it is forbidden to cry on the Sabbath. This is Jewish strength. This is almost everything I remember that has made a strong impression on me.

A scene I witnessed at Reb Osher Moishes' when he was my teacher. First, he was a miser and when the forever needy person Motl Gassus came to him to beg for a loan, no sooner did he say what he wanted than Reb Osher Moishes fell upon him with the worst expressions: "You imposter, you so-and-so, you have the nerve to come for more loans? You haven't even paid the last installment, get out of here!" Poor Motl got out meekly. As soon as Motl left the house, Reb Osher started to speak to himself: "Nu, what can he do? After all he is really a poor man and he has to support his wife and children, he must really have this loan, he has to buy goods at the marketplace." Then he asked me to run and call Motl back. When Motl returned to the house Reb Osher started to lecture him and asked him to swear that this time he would pay him on time, and gave him the loan. Reb Osher's piety won over his miserliness.

Another scene that was impressed on my memory is of Reb Yisroel Feivishes. On one of the festive occasions, Reb Yisroel was a bit late in the Synagogue, drinking a L'chayim a few times until he started to see visions. In the meantime his son who was a groom to a Wishniever girl, came and asked him to come home because the Mechutan had come. The son was a bit unhappy with his father's appearance. Reb Yisroel noticed this and remarked to his son: "So you are ashamed of your father the Shikor? So let us see - choose any Tosaphot and I will tell you the Commentary." That is how Yampoller teachers are - Reb Osher Moishes and Reb Yisroel Feivishes. My hand refuses to write more, so I will make this short. I thank you very much for your very much appreciated gift of the book.

Hershel Zuckerman

Shalom Dear Reb A. L. Gellman,

In this letter I will write about the Yampoller Reb Leibish Lerner. Leibish Lerner came to Yampol from Brody. He was one of the best students of Reb Shlomo Kluger, who is renowned as the Broder Maggid. Reb Leibish Lerner was not a great orator and I never heard him deliver a sermon for the people, not even Shabbath Shuva or Shabbath HaGadol. He was, however, considered by the Rabbis in the community to be a deep scholar. The Chassidim considered him to be a Kotsker Chassid. In his later years he was almost totally blind. I remember that when his son Meyer studied with him to become a Rabbi, I was then already participating in the slaughter and inspection ritual and I often studied in the Rabbi's house together with Meyer. We studied the laws pertaining to forbidden foods and other laws that local Rabbis had to know. We used to sit at the table and the Rabbi used to listen to how well we did and he relied on his memory. When we learned something that was incorrect, the Rabbi used to get angry: "Peasants, peasants, you are not learning correctly, there is a period!" As a matter of fact, the Rabbi's Meyer used to go with me to the slaughterhouse, especially when it was to slaughter non-kosher. In order to study the appropriate laws, he wanted to learn the practical applications not only the theoretical.

The Rabbi was not pleased with the politics that the Rebbetzen carried on with the help from the rich. He was helpless against them. This is all I can remember about the great and respectable Rabbi Leibush Lerner.

Now the week of Tammuz (June/July) is the memorial for Reb Yosef, or as he is known, the grandson of Rebbe Yi'vi, the founder of the Ostra Dynasty. His eternal place is on the New Yampoller cemetery. In the Chassidic world, Yampol was called "The Small Eretz

Yisroel" because of the great men who rested in the Yampoller cemetery.

Many old Ostra Chassidim used to come to honor his memory on his memorial day. The day did not consist only of drinking. Among them was always the Charner Rabbi, Reb Itzi and his brother Reb Chaiml, the Kornitzer Rabbi, Simcha and Reb Aba Kominker, and sometimes also my uncle Reb Berl Klinger, and many others. Ours was the designated house. The schedule for the day was as follows: quite early everyone went for Tfilah and everyone studied his daily early morning lessons. Around nine o'clock we were together at the Ostra Synagogue for open prayers. After prayers, we went to the cemetery. We said various prayers until almost dusk and then came back to our house where a fine feast had been prepared. In order that it be called a true "Mitzvah Feast" a bottle of whiskey was put on the table, as well as the big Passover samovar. With every l'chayim an "ocean of Torah was spoken." When we departed the bottle of whiskey was only half empty, but the scent of Torah was felt for many days afterwards.

With this I close writing my recollections because my doctor has forbidden me to write even a few lines. Heartfelt regards to Reuven and to all the friends who are participating in this holy work.

Comradely blessings

Hershel Zuckerman.

With G-d's help, Monday, [the week of the Torah reading of] Chukas, 5722 [1962], Chicago

Greetings my dear and important friend Mr. A.L. Gellman,

Dear Friend, you have given me a hard task. First to write and second to write about the honor and people in the town. But I have to fulfill your request. First of all there is a mistake about Yossele Bereshis as a partner to Yisroel Feivishes. It was not Yossele Bereshis but Reb Yossele Chasan who was Yisroel Feivishes' partner. They always went together and even studied together in Shul. They were called the dress with the undershirt. I will tell you a secret. The two friends studied together at midnight Nigla and Nistar [*9] It happened once that I was late in Shul and came home after midnight. I noticed a light in Yosele's Chasan's room. Out of curiosity I looked more closely and saw the two friends absorbed in study. Naturally I told my father, who has since passed away. It was no surprise to him but I had to promise my father not to reveal the secret. Naturally the circumstances are different now. I can be a witness that Reb Yossele Chasan, may he rest in peace, was constantly sitting and studying Torah except when he was scribing the Sefer Torah and a Torah he wrote with sacredness and purity. He was Rabbi Yisroel Feivishes' partner. 'Woe to that which is lost and cannot be found.'

Yossele Bereshis, with whom I studied for two seasons, inaugurated the system of distributing "Uraken" [homework] when he returned from Odessa. From him I learned the Blessing of the Moon. Psalms Chapter 110 he knew by heart. Among the scholars was Rabbi Aaron - David Gasson's son-in-law. He was a learned scholar. When he was not teaching he traveled to the markets, going from one market to another and when he returned on Thursdays very tired, especially in the winter, his best relaxation was to come to the kloiz and learn with a young man for several hours.

From Rabbi Yankel Zalman I learned grammar. He was a learned scholar in the subject of grammar and very knowledgeable in the Bible. Even though he was a great scholar he was afraid to mention the words Tanach and Grammar in front of the Trisker Chassidim and their leader Rabbi Berash Kniff. Only when the first rays of wisdom started to shine in the Yampol houses did he overcome his fear of the Trisker Chassidim.

Rabbi Eliyahu Weisstaub, the watchmaker, was very knowledgeable about Hebrew writings. He was a rare bible student, very humble and on top of it all, very poor. Being a regular guest in our home (when he was in Yampol) he once asked my father for advice. He was offered the position of Rabbi in Kaltschin(?) but he was afraid to take it because he did not know how to negotiate. I was not his pupil but we once studied the Torah reading of Haazim together for a few weeks and I have not forgotten it to this day.

A Butcher Was Reprimanded Because He Insulted the Slaughterer (Shoichet)

The story was the following: There was a tradition in Yampol that both slaughterers used to go together for the Saturday [probably Saturday night] and Sunday slaughterings. Between them they used to divide the weeks. That is, when a butcher needed something slaughtered, whichever shoichet was on that shift would take care of it. Once it happened that the butcher, Alter Avrahameles needed something slaughtered, and it happened to be Aharon Shmuel's week. Under the store where the animals were slaughtered - before there were slaughterhouses - there was a bathroom. Aharon Shmuel had to use the bathroom. The butcher's son, named Avraham Alter Avrameles, a really impudent and arrogant fellow, started banging on the floor, yelling "Shoichet, go faster!" This really seemed funny to the onlookers. Aharon Shmuel did not hurry, and went down to the river to wash his hands.

When the young fellow took hold of the head of the animal, Aharon Shmuel put away the knife and struck the younger man a couple of times, and did not want to slaughter the animal. Alter Avrahameles, Avraham's father, went to get my father to do the slaughtering. When father asked him where Aharon Shmuel was, he started to stammer. Father could tell something was not right, and refused to go until Aharon Shmuel came over. When Aharon Shmuel arrived, he told him what had happened, and about the insults he suffered. Father still refused to slaughter until Alter and his son reconciled with Aharon Shmuel.

Instead of apologizing to Aharon Shmuel, they started to insult him even more. To make a long story short, three weeks went by when the butcher had nothing to sell. He then went to the Police Commissioner in town, who was unable to help him. Finally the butcher and his son had to go to the Ostra kloiz (small shul) in stockinged feet and in public be reproached. They finally apologized to Aharon Shmuel, who forgave them. This all happened around 1901 or 1902.

Hershel Zuckerman

MY CHILDHOOD FRIEND
by Aryeh Leib Gellman

[134]
And very, very great is the pain,
There was a man and they saw: he is no more,
Before his time did this man die,
And the song of his life stopped in the middle

by H.N.Bialik

I want to shed a few tears into the glass of sorrows filled by the sudden death of the friend of my youth, Horzshach, who emigrated to Argentina in 1920 and died suddenly in Buenos Aires on October 15th 1961.

It is difficult to come to terms with the idea the cruel death was so brutal as to rob us of the best, dearest and most ideal friend that we had. It is hard to think about it but sad reality slaps one in the face and reminds one constantly that the dear close friend, whom I met four years ago in Buenos Aires, is no longer among the living. The good learned friend Jacob Horzshach is dead.

We did not see each other for fifty years but we kept in close contact by writing. Despite my troubles I wrote to him from time to time and he, the good Yankel, answered much more often. In his letters, which unfortunately I did not keep, I always found valuable thoughts. I remember only a small part of them. His mind did not know any limitations. In the small chambers of his thought process unfolded wide horizons and wide thoughts which encompassed the entire world.

In one of his letters he wrote "Man has to be free, think freely. The brain is the highest authority of mankind. This is the greatest gift of man and nobody has the right to take it away from him." For many years he was upset about our shtetl Yampol. Life in Buenos Aires obviously did not change him. He remained the introverted Yankel. He remained the man of the book. The same was as during our youth in Yampol, he was drawn back to "The Strong Hand" of RamBam. During my visit to Buenos Aires I had to promise him to send him the "The Strong Hand" His heart and his brain drew him to the old sufferings. I kept my promise. I sent him the gift but unfortunately death took him too soon, before he could enjoy the great books. In one of his letters he wrote to me: "I study "The Strong Hand" every day, just as we did once in the Yampol Shul and when I open "The Strong Hand" you are standing in front of my eyes and I mention it to my wife and children."

The tens of years that he lived in Argentina did not diminish his quest for learning. He knew Hebrew and Hebrew Literature well. He knew many languages, Russian, German, French, English and Spanish. During my visit to Argentina, I admired his knowledge of world literature.

As a learned man, he thought seriously and deeply about social and philosophical problems.

In one of his letters he expressed the following thought which, it turned out, bothered and hurt him a great deal. "The individual," he wrote, "becomes ground between the risks of life in this modern society. We put too much emphasis on collectivism. We forget the individual. Who cares these days about an individual? This is the cause of many tragedies in life because we push the individual into a corner. Collectivisim will never be cured if the individual stays in his misery and helplessness."

The idea of communism, which penetrated so deeply in many countries, did not impress him. He was not the only one who thought that way. Deep in his heart he carried the tragedies of communistic destruction brought upon this world.

Yankel Horzshach was blessed with wonderful spiritual modesty, quiet and calm. That cost him a lot in his social life. He could have played a great public role, be it as a writer or in public service, but the aforementioned characteristics held him back. Therefore he remained closed up within his own private domain.

I quote a few sentences from a eulogy which his friend Mr. Wolf Schweizer gave in Buenos Aires at the unveiling:

"It was once said that a human being resembles a tree - yes - to a tree Yankel was compared. A palm tree - tall and slim with a crown of white on his head ..."

"Yankel Horzshach was not in public service and therefore was not known publicly. Many lesser people than him were more popular. Why? Because Yankel did not want to stop learning. In the last months of his meaningful life he was very busy, with great perseverance he again studied the works of RamBam. And when he was not learning by himself, he would study with others, friends, children and grandchildren who carried on his reverence for learning.

When Yaacov Horzshach received an impressive letter from his friend A. L. Gellman, a new book or the newspaper "Hatzofeh," he used to take it to the Knesset Israel Shul so that other Jews could enjoy it. Yaacov Horzshach's memory will be etched for many years in the hearts and minds of those who knew him and his family will find consolation in his good reputation. That is the way his new friends in Argentina thought about him.

But besides the aforementioned spiritual characteristics, deep in his heart he loved the Jewish people.

The land of Israel, Zionism and Hebrew were the Holy of Holies of his life. Talking to him I felt the holy fire burning in his heart. Every one of his letters was glowing with love for Israel and ended with heartfelt greetings for the old-new Jerusalem. "Shalom Jerusalem our old and holy city, blessed that you were privileged to live there and breath its air" was the ending of his letter to me.

With regard to Hebrew, it is really a pity that he neglected to participate in the Hebrew press. The difficult economic conditions he endured in Argentina were actually the reasons. His Hebrew letters contained a wonderful style as well as content. I submit that Yaacov Horzshach was a great expert on the Hebrew language and literature. With him a brilliant Hebrew writer was lost.

The light of a dear friend was snuffed. The warm Jewish heart stopped beating suddenly.

Lie in peace, dear friend, may the earth be sweet to you.

AN EVALUATION OF MY FATHER
(Of Blessed Memory)
by Sonya Horzshach

[137]

Mr. A.L. Gellman, Shalom,

My mother and I were extremely concerned a few months ago when Mr.Finkelstein told us about your health situation. Unfortunately, it wasn't possible for him to personally send you the news, the grievous news, about which you now know. We read your first letter both with apprehension and with relief. Thank G-d you all arrived in peace. Mother has answered you. She got the letter that you mentioned. Now, a little belatedly, let me respond in my poor Yiddish to try to briefly characterize the personality of my dear father of blessed memory, who passed away in Buenos Aires, Argentina on the 5th of Cheshvan 5722 (October 15, 1961.)

The books you recently sent are right in front of me on my desk, as well as a letter you gave me a couple of years ago, when you were vacationing in Buenos Aires. It is dated in 1911, and is fifty years old. Your friend from your youth sent it to you to New York from Yampol. When I compare the handwriting with that on the letter you have in my father's handwriting, it seems as if it were just yesterday. I am absolutely positive, without any hesitation whatsoever, that this is the same hand that started writing fifty years ago, and nothing on the paper is missing. The youthful grace and elegance remained to his last years. My father's moral personality comes across clearly on paper, as well as his firm, strong and sure philosophical principles. Goodness and integrity and grace are three fundamental aspects of his character. I don't think he ever had an evil memory. Jabotinsky once wrote about people with "black memories" and people with "white memories." Father belonged to the latter; never did anything evil stay in his memory. He always would remember all the good aspects of every person and every situation.

With regard to his mastery of Hebrew and his capacity to learn, an acquaintance of his, Wolf Switzer, is going to write to you about this, since I am not equipped to give my opinion and am not familiar with this aspect of my father. I often remember, however, how he would frequently come to my rescue when, as a university student, I had a difficult problem in advanced mathematics. In his final years he used to have a wonderful simplicity in his way of thinking. He considered money and personal profit to be of little importance, something that is certainly not a contemporary idea! Father was a tolerant person, however, and perfectly understood the practical needs of others. He was perhaps an overly modest person. He was often invited to take a leading role in various national organizations, credit cooperatives or

Talmud Torah schools; he always refused. This wasn't, heaven forbid, because of some inferiority complex. He always stayed away from controversy and stayed close to his family, children and books.

Mr. Gellman, there is much that could be written about my father, and yet I find it a bit hard to write easily about the past. The memories run into each other, as if each one would like to be the first mentioned. They dull my mind and keep me from writing. Your were a real member of our family, and father mentioned you often, on many occasions. You can be sure that you had a great and true friend who has now so suddenly and unexpectedly passed away.

Yampol is a separate chapter in my father's life, something that you certainly know more about than I do. Yampol, a strange word, the name of a small forgotten and ignored town; I can connect very closely to the sound YAMPOLE. It tumbles out of my mouth every time I hear the name. It is remarkable how often my lips murmur the word Yampol. Yampol ...and tears flow slowly together. I should mention that fact that I was born there, and on the same letter that you gave me is inscribed my grandfather's name, which is my name.

You asked me, Mr. Gellman, whether anything about Father has been written in newspapers. Let me answer you by saying that a number of friends have asked the same question, and as far as I know, someone had wanted to print something, but nothing came of it. In my opinion, it is better that way!

The newspapers are full of 'necrologs,' the 'eulogy-makers,' who used to be around in Jewish life, are still around today, and will probably be around tomorrow - they specialize in writing about the dead.

Their whole job only revolves around those who have already breathed their last. Such necrologs usually get excited and empowered from exaggeration. The dead who are written about appear as great bright figures, with all kinds of great qualities, fine qualities and nobility, which they use to describe every person who qualify to be a dead person. According to their style you notice only a conventional and formal approach. I ask myself: Who knew Father so well and thoroughly to be able to permit something about him to be written? In my opinion, you are the only person capable of doing this. All of us who loved him so much and who feel his unforgettable loss at every moment would be grateful to you for doing it. We are thoroughly convinced that you alone are capable to describe a person "who was respectable with himself, who did not fool himself about what he felt in his own heart, who started crying only when tears made him cry, and who concealed his grief. This is the kind of man he was, if not a saint; he was a truly honest person."

Yours truly,

Sonia Horzshach

NOTATIONS
MAY G-D REMEMBER...
by David Rubin

[141]

The souls of our brothers, sisters and relatives in the town of Yampol (Volhyn region) who died, were murdered, and who sacrificed their lives for the sanctification of G-d's name, during the Holocaust and Annihilation in 1943-1944 under the accursed murderers, may their names and memory be obliterated.

May the souls of the holy and pure ones be bound up with the lives of the nation, together with the souls of all the righteous men and women. May G-d remember them for goodness among the rest of the holy ones, the murdered of the Jewish People, and may He take revenge for the spilled blood.

The list of the dead and murdered families has been compiled by David Rubin

LETTER TO WORLD UNION OF EMIGRES

[150]

WORLD UNION OF VOLHYNIA EMIGRES
Office in Israel,
Tel Aviv, Antokolsky Street 15,
Apartment of Zvi Berger,
POB 242.

To all Volhynia emigré organizations ['Landsmanshaften']:

In a great period in world history and during the revival of the Jewish People in our generation, we turn to you, the Volhynia emigrés, worldwide, and call upon you from Israel. Be bold, and stretch out your hand to join with our Volhynia World Union to erect the monument to the memory of the destroyed Volhynia communities, their leaders, heads, thinkers, poets, rabbis, activists, politicians, and all Jews who lived, and worked in the once ardent homeland - in Volhynia.

We are trying to build a monumental culture center "Heichal Volhynia" [Volhynia Center] in which we can collect all the products of intellectual life of Volhynia Jewry for around 1000 years, until the Nazi Destruction.

Heichal Volhynia should serve as a center for all Volhynia Jews and their emigré organizations. It should serve as the repository of the past, of the golden Jewish bonds of Volhynia and the priceless output for our People and our country, for our generation and generations to come, who will be able to find in it a source of education and development.

Heichal Volhynia will be used for social and cultural activities, by academies, exhibits, libraries, archives, seminars, artistic activities and courses, performances, sports and other activities.

Heichal Volhynia will manage the worldwide Volhynia file system by which anyone interested may look for relatives and friends from Volhynia, and thereby enable them to search for lost siblings, acquaintances and others, with information about them.

Heichal Volhynia will house the appropriate monument of our martyrs of the 160 Volhynia communities and the heroic resistance in some of them. It will be possible to make dedications to emigré and other organizations, groups and individuals in various ways, and to have them published in a special dedication book, etc.

A Volhynia encyclopedia will be published by the World Union, which will collect the Yizkor books of the communities as well as other works published by historians.

A worldwide congress of Volhynia Jews from the entire world will be held in Heichal Volhynia as soon as the appropriate accommodations are arranged.

The Union is currently preparing a collection of memoirs about Volhynia culled from historical announcements and notices, which would be of interest to every emigré.

We are aware of the many memorials already dedicated in various places, which are sacred and priceless. Our undertaking is for the entire Volhynia emigré community with the possibility of making special provisions for particular communities here in Israel, including the aforementioned memorials.

Our call has been warmly received by Volhynia emigré organizations. Their tangible assistance and cooperation gives us the hope that our project is proper and necessary.

Friends, get involved in our sacred task.

With friendly greetings,
The World Union of Volhynia Emigrés

Necrology

The Saints/Martyrs from Yampol, the district of Volhyn, who were murdered by the Nazis
(May their name [Nazis] be erased and their memory, too).

Abeles	Family of Berel Yoel Abeles
Abners	Family of Yossi Abners
Aharon	Son of my brother in-law Aharon the slaughterer and checker
Alter	Family of Alter: Rabbi Dodis Azriel, Baruch and their sisters.
Altereche	Family of the widow Altereche
Ashers (Kessel??)	Family of Yisroel Ashers (Kessel??)
Asnat	Family of Lipa Asnat
Asnat	Family of Leibene Asnat
Avraham	Family of Avraham Yehuda
Avraham	Family of Shmuel Avraham (tailor and Torah reader)
Azriel	Family of Azriel son of the widow Breina
Babas	Family of Itzi Babas
Badner	Family of Aryeh Badner
Baranick	Family of Moshe Baranick
Barles	Family of Zeida Barles the son in law of Rebbe Yisroel Feiveshes and his wife Rachel
Barles	Family of Barles Grandson of Rebbe Yisreol Feiveshes
Ber	Family of Binem Ber
Bereshes	Family of Yossele Bereshes
Berger	Family of Shmuel Berger
Berger	Family of Avraham Berger
Bernstein	Family of Moshe Bernstein
Bernstein	Family of Moshe Bernstein from Techemlie
Blecher	Family of Yosef Blecher
Blecher	Family of Moshe Blecher
Boibe	Family of Boibe the hipacrit

Bonemas	Family of Velvel Bonemas and Heitman?
Borstein (Disnitzkis)	Family of Velvel Borstein (who is called Disnitzkis)
Borvitsch	Family of Itzi Borvitsch
Breiness	Family of Zalman Breiness
Bridyage	Family of Yaacov Bridyage
Chaim	Family of Chaim Ben David
Chaim	Family of Chaim from the ???? (in yiddish)
Chaim	Family of his son in-law Reuben
Chaimless	Family of Avraham Rebbe Chaimless
Chait	Family of Moshe Perles Chait
Chait	Family of the sons of Matti Chait
Chalaf	Family of Yossi Chalaf
Chalaf	Family of Yisroel Chalaf
Chana	Family of Chana Lieba the Seamstress (?? Yiddish - Shenayderka)
Chanas	Family of Bonim Aaron Chanas
Chava	Family of Chava Shaindel & her husband, Zaidel
Chayes	Family of Azriel Shmuel Chayes
Chazan	Family of Yosel Chazan
Chazan	Family of Rabbi Pesah Chazan, Rabbi Fischel the son-in-law (a judge).
David	Family of Hershel Chaim David from founders of the Zionist group in the city
David	Family of Hershel son in-law of Chaim David
Doodi	Family of the Dayan Rav Doodi, of blessed memory
Dricker	Family of Binem Dricker
Eideles	Family of Issac Eideles
Ekav (Yaacov)	Family of Moshe Ekav (Yaacov)
Elihus	Family of Yosel Elihus (the teacher)
Eliyas	Family of Eingel Eliyas
Eliyas	Family of Moishlah Eliyas

Esther	Family of Esther the midwife
Fankevitzer	Family of Avraham Fankevitzer
Feivishes	Family of Yisroel Feivishes
Feivishis	Family of Azriel (his son in-law)
Feivishis	Family of Lazel Feivishis
Feldman	Family of Moshe and Esther Feldman
Fiegeleches	Family of the widow Hentze Fiegeleches
Figer	Family of Chaim Figer, his wife Sarah and their daughters.
Fitzis /Pitzis	Family of David Shaindel Fitzis /Pitzis
Flam	Family of Sender Flam
Fonkevitch	Family of Yudel Fonkevitch
Friedman	Family of Anshell Friedman
Garberg	Family of Yosef Garberg and his family
Gassi	Family of the widow Gassi
Gassis	Family of Aharon David (son in-law of Gassis)
Gassis	Family of Mattel Gassis
Gat	Family of Yankel Gat
Gat	Family of Matti Gat
Gele	Family of Gele
Gerberg	Family of Hershel Gerberg
Gerberg	His wife Baibe, and their daughters Bayla, Malka Toiba?
Gitles	Family of Yankel Gitles
Gittelman	Family of Moshe Gittelman
Greenberg	Family of Shmuel Greenberg
Greenstein	Family of Peretz Greenstein
Guberman	Family of Head of the Kahal (community of the city of Yamel) our teacher the rav Shmuel Guberman of blessed memory, who was killed in a strange way by the Nazis (may their name be erased).
Haber	Family of Haber son of the Rav
Hazakan	Family of Rebbe Yehuda Leib Hazakan (name or / the elder)

Hazkan	Family of sons of Toivel Hazkan (name or / the elder)
Hershel	Family of Hershel from the wall
Hillel	Family of Rebbe Hillel and his wife Chana
Hindes	Family of Haim and Chaya Hindes son in-law of Lezel
Horzshach	Shmuel Horzshach son-in-law of Hershel Gerberg
Horzshach	Family of Sanny Horzshach
Issacs	Family of Simcha Chaim Issacs
Kakeshes	Family of Moshe Kakeshes
Karlinishke	Family of Rachel Karlinishke. Her son of Yosef and daughter Esther Feige
Karpin	Family of Avraham Karpin and his son, Tzvi (Hirschel)
Kartman	Family of David Kartman
Kavel	Family of Ephraim Kavel
Kemmelmacher	Family of Berel Kemmelmacher
Kertman	Family Shmelke son of Noah Kertman,
Kertman	Family of Yisroel Kertman. Itta Toiba Saraes, Chaya, her daugther; Chaim Leib, & Noah
Kesselman	Family of Nechemiah Kesselman
Kesselman	Family of Simcha and Channah Kesselman
Ketzeles	Family of Moshe Ketzeles the Shoemaker
Ketzeles	Family of Shlomo Ketzeles.
Kirzshener	Family of Yisroel Kirzshener
Kniff	Family of Pinni son of Baruch Kniff
Kniff	Family of Barish Kniff
Kniff	Family of Simcha son of Baruch Kniff
Kotlier	Family of Mendel Kotlier
Krupnik	Family of Berel Krupnik
Labishkes	Family of Simcha Labishkes from outside the city
Lerner	Fievel Lerner, son-in-law of Hershel

	Gerberg
Lerner	Family of Shalom Lerner
Lerner	Family of the Rav Meir Lerner
Lerner	Family of Chaim Shalom Lerner
Lerner	Family of Yankel Lerner & wife Hannah
Lerner	Family of Feivel Shalom Lerner
Leib	Family of Dackman Hirsh Leib
Lielka	Family of Moshe Lielka (Tailor)
Mak	Family of David Mak
Makrofedereni	Family of Yehezkel Makrofedereni
Mallin	Family of Shaul Mallin
Manies	Family of Avraham Manies
Manies	Family of Yossel Manies
Maskaliveker	Family of Shmelke Maskaliveker
Matya	Family of Iytzi Matya (the butcher and Torah reader)
Meister	Family of Eliyahu Zeiger Meister
Melach	Family of Yossel Melach
Melamed	Family of Rebbe Yankel Melamed
Melamed	Family of Natan Melamed
Melamed	Family of Nachman Melamed
Melamed	Family of Eliezer Melamed
Melamed	Family of Yehezkel Melamed
Melamed	Family of Yoel Melamed, his wife Bayla Toibe
Melamed	Family of Ephraim Melamed
Melamed	Hoddel daughter of Rebbe Zanweil Melamed and his family
Miazevetz	Family of Baruch Miazevetz
Mikelisher	Family of Meir Mikelisher
Mishecheralnik	Family of Wolf Mishecheralnik
Mitshnik	Family of Aharon Mitshnik
Mordecai	Family of Mordecai Yaacov and sons
Moshes	Family of Asher Moshes
Nachum	Family of Rebbe Nachum Shlomo
Peretz	Family of Peretz the doctor
Pinchas	Family of Pinchas (the water drawer)

Ratzes	Family of David Ratzes
Reiles	Family of Babe Reiles
Reuben	Family of David Reuben. His sister Zippie. His sister Malka. Brother-in-law Aaron (who is a slaughterer and checker) husband of Malka. Brother in law Mavikotz Dudi. His daughters Miriam, Malka, Tammy, Toiba & Chayka. Daughters of Aharon, Toiba and Malka.
Reuben	Family of Yosef Reuben. His wife Faggie (Fanny). His daughter Tzirel (Tzili).
Roitman	Family of Yankel Roitman
Rozenberg	Family of Benyamin Rozenberg and his wife Sarah and their children Chayake and Leahke
Saraes	Family of Ita Toibe Saraes
Sarahkes?	Family of Menny Sarahkes?
Sares / Shares	Family of Chaim Sares / Shares
Scheinder	Family of David Scheinder
Shabbathai	Family of Shabbathai the water drawer.
Shabses	Family of Elinka Shabses
Sharas	Family of Issac Toiba Sharas
Sharhas	Family of Yitzak Toyba Sharhas and Esther Itta his wife (double???)
Shaul	Family of Shaul the Toieber
Shayer	Family of Azriel Shayer
Shemesh	Family of Moshe Shemesh
Shemesh	Family of Simcha Shemesh
Shenapper	Brother of his wife Sani Shenapper
Sherer	Family of Michal Sherer
Shetz	Family of Michal Shetz and his mother Leah.
Shifargal	Family of Bertzi Shifargal and his wife Hannah and daughter Devorah.
Shimonis	Family of Shmuel Aharon Shimonis
Shimons	Family of Mati Shimons (the butcher)
Shmuel	Family of Rav Aharon Shmuel (slaughterer and checker)

Shmueles	Family of Yitzchak Aharon Shmueles (slaughterer and checker)
Shoichet (Yisroelis)	Family of Michal Shoichet (Yisroelis)
Shuster	Family of Issikel Shuster
Shuster	Family of Shmuel Shuster
Sifarad	Family of Rav Meir Sifarad
Sifarad	Family of Mattel (his son in-law)
Silke	Family of Silke
Silkes	Family of Shlomo Silkes
Silkes	Family of Avraham Silkes
Silkes	Family of Yehoshua Silkes
Sivker	Family of Shimon Sivker
Slaves (Melamed)	Family of Yaacov Slaves (Melamed)
Sofer	Family of Pesach Sofer
Staliar	Family of Shlomo Staliar
Staliar	Family of Yisroel Staliar
Tabatshnik	Family of Yoel Tabatshnik
Tachman	Family of Yisroel Rivem Tachman
Tachman	Family of Aharon Shimon Tachman
Tandetnik	Family of Zeida Tandetnik
Tatte	Family of Moshe Tatte
Tevel	Family of Tevel the elder
Tscharnes	Family of Zisi Tscharnes
Tzedukes	Family of Yankel Tzedukes
Tzigeles	Family of Meir Tzigeles
Tzines	Family of Mendel Saphra Tzines
Tzinker	Family of Issac Tzinker
Tzvihes	Family of Mordechai Moshe Tzvihes
Tzvik	Family of Baruch Tzvik
Varevedekir	Family of Nachum Varevedekir
Weiners	Family of Yankel Aharon Weiners
Weissberg	Family of Michal Weissberg
Weitzman	Family of Zeide Shimeliches Weitzman
Weitzman	Rav Yanakele Weitzman, Rav from Greydineg
Yahalom	Family of Yahalom

Yankel	Family of Rav Yankel from Maver
Yankel	Family of Rebbe Yankel (from the wall)
Yankeleches	Family of son in-law of Avraham Yankeleches
Yankeleches	Family of Avraham Yankeleches, the butcher)
Yankeleches	Family of his brother Iytzi Yankeleches
Yehuda	Family of Avraham Yehuda, (the butcher)
Yeishia	Family of Yeishia from the Mihal?
Yekutiel	Family of Chaim Yekutiel
Yischares	Family of Zeidel Yischares
Yisroel	Family of Rabbi Yisroel (Shoichet U'bodek - slaughterer and checker, to check to see if it is kosher)
Yitzchak	Family of Leib Hirsch Yitzchak and Matti and their wives.
Yossel	Family of Yossel a judge and teacher of law
Yossi	Family of Yossi the wagon owner
Zanvil	Family of Rabbi Zanvil (Either name or teacher)

Original Necrology

א שטעטל אין פלאממען

הקדושים ביאמפאלע, פלך ווהלין, שנהרגו ע"י הנאצים ימח שמם וזכרם

משפחת בעריש קניף

משפחת עזריאל שמואל חייעס

משפחת דוד קערטמן

משפחת יואל טאבאטשניק

משפחת סנדר פלאם

משפחת בנימין ראזענבערג ואשתו שרה

משפחת פרץ גרינשטיין

ובנותיהם: חיה'קע ולאה'קע

משפחת ברוך צוויק

משפחת עזריאל שער

משפחת חיים שלום לערנער

משפחת האלמנה אלטערעכע

משפחת יאנקעל לערנער ואשתו חנה

משפחת יוסף בלעכער

משפחת ישעיה פון דער מיהל

משפחת בערל קרופניק

משפחת אפרים קאוואל

משפחת משה בלעכער

משפחת דוד מאק

משפחת מענדיל קאטליער

משפחת משה איקעב (יעקב)

משפחת אריה באדנער

משפחת חיים יקותיאל

משפחת בינעם דריקער

משפחת נחום וואריוועדקיר

משפחת איצי מאטיע שמעונס קצב ובעל קורא

משפחת מיכל שוחט (ישראליס)

משפחת שמואל אברהם חיט ובעל קורא

משפחת אשר משה'ס

משפחת אברהם יענקלעבכעס, קצב

משפחת משה ליאלקע (חיט)

משפחת אחיו איצי יענקלעבכעס

משפחת שמואל אהרן שמעונים

משפחת ישראל פייוישעס

משפחת וואלף טשעכראלניק

משפחת עזריאל חתנו

משפחת זעלוויל בורשטיין

משפחת מאטי שמעונס, קצב

(המכונה דיסניצקי'ס)

משפחת אברהם יהודה, קצב

משפחת ליפא אסנת

משפחת פנחס שואב מים

משפחת בינעם בער

משפחת סאני האראוישעך

משפחת יעקב ברידיאגע

משפחת אנשיל פרידמן

משפחת לייבענע אסנת

משפחת ישראל קערטמאן

משפחת זיידע טאנדעטניק

משפחת ברוך מיאזוועעץ

משפחת חוה שיינדל ובעלה זיידעל

משפחת הדיין ר' דודי ז"ל

משפחת חנה ליבע די שניידערקע

משפחת לאזל פייייששיס

משפחת יחזקאל מקרופעדערני

משפחת יאנקל רויטמן

משפחת יאנקעל גיטלעס

משפחת אהרון מיטשניק

משפחת איטה טויבע שרה'ס

משפחת שמחה חיים אייזיקס

משפחת יענקל גאט

משפחת דאקמן הירש ליב

משפחת מאטי גאט

משפחת אייזיק אידעלס

משפחת ישראל ריוועם טאכמן

משפחת יוסל מלאך

משפחת אהרן שמעון טאכמן

יאמפאלער פינקס

משפחת בויבע הצבועה	משפחת האלמנה גאסי.
משפחת יוסף גארבערג ומשפחתו	משפחת דוד ראצעס
משפחת בערצי, שפארגאל ואשתו חנה,	משפחת דוד שיינדל פיציס
ובתם דבורה	משפחת הערשל מן החומה
משפחת חיים פיגור ואשתו שרה ובתם	משפחת מענדל שפרה צינעס
משפחת ועלוויל בונעמס והייטמאן	משפחת מאיר ציגעלעס
משפחת יואל מלמד, אשתו בילה טויבה	משפחת שמואל שוסטער
משפחת משה באראניק	משפחת הרב מאיר לערנער
משפחת ר' יאנקל פון מאוער	משפחת יוסילע בערישעס
משפחת ר' זאנוויל מלמד	משפחת ר' ישראל שו״ב
משפחת אפרים מלמד	משפחת יוסל חזן
משפחת ר' אהרן שמואל שו״ב	משפחת ישראל סטאליאר
משפחת שלום לערנער	משפחת אליהו זייגער מייסטער
משפחת משה בערנשטיין, פון טעכעמליע	משפחת שואל מאלין
משפחת יאסעל מאניעס	משפחת שמואל בערגער
משפחת אברהם מאניעס	משפחת אברהם בערגער
משפחת יצחק אהרן שמואלס, שו״ב	משפחת מרדכי משה צביהס
משפחת יהלום	משפחת פייוול שלום לערנער
משפחת משה גיטעלמאן	משפחת רב מאיר ספרד
משפחת מיכל וייסבערג	משפחת מאטל חתנו
משפחת ראש הקהל מעיר יאמפאלע	משפחת יוסל אליהוס מלמד
מו״ה שמואל גובערמן ז״ל שנהרג במיתה	משפחת סילקע
משונה ע״י הנאצים ימ״ש	משפחת געלע
משפחת הערשל חיים דוד מן המיסדים	משפחת אהרן דוד חתן גאסי׳
של החברה הציונית בעיירה	משפחת מאטל גאסיס
משפחת הערשל חתן חיים דוד	משפחת שלומה סילקעס
משפחת ר' יאנקעלע וייצמאן	משפחת אברהם סילקעס
הרב מגריידינג	משפחת יהושע סילקעס
משפחת יאנקעל אהרן ווינערס	משפחת ישראל אשרס (קעסל)
משפחת אייזקעל שוסטער	משפחת לייב הערש יצחק ומאטיע עם
משפחת עזריאל בן האלמנה בריינה	נשיהם
משפחת משה בערענשטיין	משפחת נחמיה קעסלמן
משפחת שמעלקע מאסקאליוונקער	משפחת שמחה וחנה קעסלמן
משפחת באבע ריילעס	משפחת מעני שרהקעס
משפחת האלמנה הענצע פויגעלעכעס	משפחת טעוול הזקן
משפחת דוד שניידער	משפחת אברהם קארפין ובנו צבי (הירשל)

151   א ש ט ע ט ל א י ן פ ל א מ ע ן

משפחת שלמה קעצעלעס

משפחת מיכל שץ, אמו לאה

משפחת ר' פסח חזן

ר' פישל חתנו של הדיין

משפחת אלתר ר' דודיס

עזריאל, ברוך ואחותם

משפחת זיידע בערלס חתנו של ר'

ישראל פייוווישעס ואשתו רחל

משפחת בושקע נכד ר' ישראל פייוווישעס

משפחת יוסי בעל עגלה

האדעל בת ר' זאנוויל מלמד ומשפחתה

משפחת זיידעל ישכר'ס

משפחת פרץ הרופא

משפחת ר' הלל ואשתו חנה

משפחת ר' נחום שלמה

משפחת ר' חיים בן דוד

משפחת ר' משה קאקעשעס

משפחת בערל קעמעלמאבער

משפחת משהלע אליהס

משפחת יוסי אבנרס

משפחת איצי בורביטש

משפחת שבתי שואב מים

משפחת בערל יואל אבאלעס

משפחת אלינקע שאבסעס

משפחת אליעזר מלמד

משפחת הייבער בן הרב

משפחת יוסל דיין ומו"ץ

משפחת משה טאטע

משפחת יחזקאל מלמד

משפחת פסה סופר

משפחת מיכל שערער

משפחת זיסיא טשארנגעס

משפחת שמואל גרינברג

משפחת משה שמש

משפחת שמחה שמש

משפחת אברהם יהודה

משפחת יוסי חלף

משפחת ישראל חלף

משפחת נחמן מלמד

משפחת אברהם ר' חיים'לעס

משפחת דוד רובין

אחותו ציפיע

אחותו מלכה

גיסו אהרון שו"ב בעל של מלכה

גיסו דודי מביקאווף

בתו מרים, מלכה, טעמי, טויבע, חייקע

בנותיו של אהרון שו"ב

טויבע, ומלכה

משפחת יוסף רובין

רעיתו פייגע (פאני)

בתו צירל (צילי)

אחות של רעיתו סאני שנאפער

משפחת זלמן בריינעס

משפחת ר' יאנקעל (מן החומה)

משפחת הירשל גארבארג

אשתו באבא, בנותיהם:

בילה, מלכה טויבה,

חתנם — פייוויל לערנער,

שמואל הורזשעך.

משפחת שמעלקע בן נח קערטמאן —

איטה טויבה שרה'ס חיה בתה, חיים

ליב, נח.

משפחת איצי באבעס

משפחת משה ואסתר פעלדמאן

משפחת אינגעל אליה'ס

משפחת יאנקעל צדוק'ס

משפחת יעקב סלאוועס (מלמד)

משפחת חיים שרהקעס

משפחת אייזיק צינקער

משפחת חתנו ראובן

משפחת משה קעצעלעס (סנדלר)

משפחת חיים פון דער ארענדא

יאמפאלער פינקס

משפחת שלמה סטאליאר

משפחת שואל דער טויבער

משפחת פיני בן ברוך קניף

משפחת שמחה בן ברוך קניף

משפחת אברהם פאנקעוויצער

משפחת מרדכי יעקב בניו

משפחת יודיל פאנקעוויץ

משפחת שמעון סיווקער

משפחת שמחה לעבישקעס מחוץ לעיר

משפחת חיים חיה הינדעס גיסו של
לאזל

משפחת בניה של גיסי אהרן שו״ב:
אברהם ויצחק

משפחת בונעם אהרן חנה׳ס

משפחת אייזיק טויבה שרה׳ס

משפחת יצחק טויבה שרה׳ס
ואסתר איטה רעיתו.

משפחת רחל קארלינטשקע
בנה יוסף ובתה אסתר פיגה

משפחת ר׳ יאנקעל מלמד.

משפחות נתן מלמד

משפחת משה פערלס חיט

משפחת בנו מאטי חיט

משפחת זיידע שימעליכעס וייצמאן

משפחת ישראל קירזשנער

משפחת חתנו של אברהם יאנקעלעכעס

משפחת אסתר המילדת

משפחת בנו של טייוועל הזקן

משפחת ר׳ יהודה ליב הזקן

משפחת מאיר מיקליאשער

ומשפחות של כל הנהרגים והנשרפים
ששמותיהם בלתי־נודעים.

Index

Note that the names in the Necrology are not indexed here.

Please search the Necrology separately starting on page 140.

NOTATIONS

1. **Chalitzah Shoe:** When a man dies and leaves no children the Torah requires his widow to either marry his brother ["yibum"] or perform the mitzvah of chalitzah. [Ashkenazic law requires specifically chalitza and not yibum.] Chalitzah consists of reading certain verses of the Torah which deal with this matter, the widow unties and removes the brother-in-law's shoes and spits toward him. There are certain halachic requirements regarding the form of the shoe and therefore every Bet Din has a shoe specifically made for this purpose.

2. **Atseres:** Shmini Atseres – The eighth day of Sukkoth.

3. **Pidyon** is an amount of money which is given to the tzadik by which he can "sweeten" harsh decrees from on high. Some rebbes did not keep the pidyonos for themselves but distributed them to the needy.

4. Simon **Petlura** ruled the Ukraine for a brief period when it was an independent republic. Between 1918-1920 he led the Pogroms and after the Soviets defeated the Ukrainian forces he fled to Paris. He was brought to trial but assassinated by Sholem Schwartzbard in 1926.

5. **Vitzmah Furnkah**: Chassidim and sefardim add this to the kaddish. It is not in the text used by mitnagdim. The entire phrase is "Vayatzmach purkanei vikarev meshichei" which is Aramaic for "and may He make His redemption bloom and may He bring close His messiah."

6. A **straw hat** was considered a sign of modernity and "enlightenment."

7. **"That person"** is a euphemism for Jesus. Even though the text says "the gentile New Year" it really means Christmas, called "Nittel" in Yiddish, when it is customary not to study Torah during the first half of the night.

8. **"The Kind sat on His throne"** is the point in the morning prayers of Rosh Hashana and Yom Kippur when the main Chazan takes over leading the prayers, just before Borchu.

9. **Nigla and Nestar**: Nigla is the revealed Torah as opposed to Nistar, the hidden Torah i.e. Kabbalah.

Jewish Headstone in the river in Yampol
(Not in the Original Yizkor Book)
Photo by Dr. Boris Khaimovich, 1999
"Courtesy of the Center for Jewish Art, Hebrew University of Jerusalem"

The cemetery of Yampol was destroyed by the army in the 1920s and the stones were thrown into the water. Researchers were fortunate to be present when the water level was low and were able to document a few of the stones. They found about twenty tombstones from the mid-eighteenth to early nineteenth century, beautifully decorated with motifs of griffins, birds, bears, and grapes.

YAMPOL July 2003
(Not in the Original Yizkor Book)

Photos by Ronald D. Doctor and Kenneth J. Doctor
(Not in original Yizkor Book)

Ronald and Kenneth Doctor visited their ancestral town of Yampol in July 2003 and discovered a new building (an Ohel) erected over the grave sites of two Rabbis. They were told that a man named "Moishe" from New York paid for the construction. Construction was completed just one week before they visited. Three weeks before their visit, the workmen, on their own initiative, retrieved 25 matzevot (headstones) that had been thrown into the river by the Soviets during communist rule

Yampol road sign

Matzevot (headstones) recovery site on the River Goryn

Rescued Matsevot (headstones) lying on the banks of the river Goryn

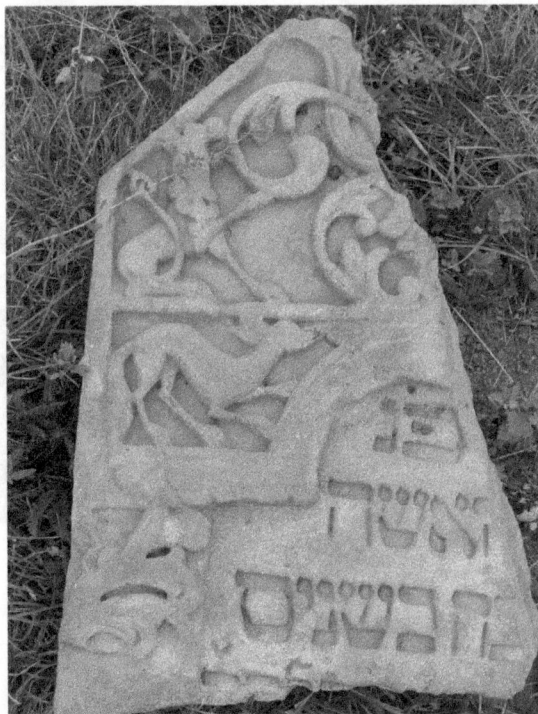

Details of the Matzevot (headstones) rescued from the River Goryn

Newly Built Ohel at Yampol Cemetery

Gate of Tsvi Kestenbaum
Donated by his sons
Dr. Eliezer *N"Y*
and Dr.Moshe Aharon *N"Y*

N"Y is the abbreviation of "Neiro Yair," which in Hebrew means:
"His candle will illuminate"

.